STUDIES IN ECONOMICS

Edited by Charles Carter

Vice-Chancellor, University of Lancaster

6

Monetary Management
Principles and Practice

STUDIES IN ECONOMICS

G. L. S. Shackle Expectation, Enterprise and Profit
J. Wilczynski The Economics of Socialism
M. Capstick The Economics of Agriculture
A. P. McAnally Economics of the Distributive Trades
K. D. George Industrial Organization: Competition, Growth and Structural Change

in preparation

R. C. Tress The Public Sector and the Private Sector
R. J. Ball Macroeconomic Planning
Hans Singer and Caroline Miles The Rich and the Poor Countries
J. G. Corina Wages and Earnings
Ian Bowen Demography and Economics
F. S. Brooman Money and Financial Institutions
G. A. Phillips and R. T. Maddock The Economic Development of Britain, 1918–1968
A. I. MacBean The Institutions of International Trade
R. D. C. Black The History of Economic Thought
Charles Kennedy The Distribution of the Product
Theo Cooper Economic Aspects of Social Security
Gavin McCrone Economic Integration
A. J. Brown Regional Economics
W. J. L. Ryan Demand
D. J. Horwell International Trade Theory
E. J. Mishan Cost-Benefit Analysis

Monetary Management

Principles and Practice

BY

A. B. CRAMP

Fellow of Emmanuel College, Cambridge

London

GEORGE ALLEN & UNWIN LTD

RUSKIN HOUSE MUSEUM STREET

First published in 1971

ISBN 0 04 332043 0 cased
ISBN 0 04 332044 9 paper

Printed in Great Britain
10 on 11 point Times Roman
by Alden & Mowbray Ltd
Osney Mead, Oxford

EDITOR'S NOTE

Economics is a large and rapidly developing subject, and needs, as well as elementary works for the beginner, authoritative textbooks on special subjects. This book belongs to a series of such textbooks (more than forty titles are planned); the general level is that of the second or third year in a British university course, but the books are written so as to be intelligible to other readers with a particular interest in the subject concerned

C.F.C.

PREFACE

The main concern of this book is to examine anew the orthodox economic theory concerning the techniques of central bank control over the monetary system in the interests of stabilization policy. To this end, one major thread of the exposition consists of explanation of abstract *principles*; a major part of the contribution of economics to policy-making is that it helps to reduce the bewildering complexity of economic behaviour to an order which is at least conceptually manageable. But the other major thread is the constant attempt to test these principles by reference to their outworking in *practice* in a realistic institutional setting.

Just because the world is so complex and untidy, policy actions are governed by abstract theories (whether explicit or implicit). It is therefore important that these theories should be as valid and realistic as we can make them. Academic economists tend to prize in their theories the qualities of precision and rigour. Precision and rigour are rightly regarded as the enemies of loose and inconsistent thinking, but they can also be enemies of realism. Economists too readily throw out the baby of realism with the bath water of woolliness. In this book the attempt is made (with what success must be judged by others) to use theory while giving realism priority over rigour.

Because this is a small book on a big subject it necessarily assumes some initial knowledge. It is directed primarily to economics students, from middle undergraduate level onwards, who already possess some knowledge both of macroeconomic theory and of the United Kingdom banking and financial systems.

Chapter 2 draws heavily on my article in *Lloyds Bank Review*, October 1967, and I am grateful for the editor's permission to re-use some of the material from it.

Without wishing to implicate anyone, I should like to acknowledge debts to the published writings of R. S. Sayers, A. N. McLeod, H. Minsky and M. J. Artis; to some unpublished work by J. Dawson; to postal discussion with A. Lonie and to personal discussion with P. Herrington; and to helpful suggestions by the Editor of this series, C. F. Carter. The influence of my two-year secondment to the Bank of England in 1963–5 will be obvious to any of my academic colleagues who might chance to read these pages.

April 1970 A. B. CRAMP

CONTENTS

CHAPTER 1

The Conceptual Framework

There was a stage in the evolution of analytical economics during which it was fashionable to regard money as a veil concealing the operation of the fundamental processes that were regarded as the theorist's true concern. This notion rings strange to the lay student of affairs, likely to be impressed with the pervasive importance of finance in all aspects of economic activity. Whatever the changing emphases as economists continue to debate the relative *strength* of 'real' and 'financial' influences on aggregate demand and output, and however much some may regard lay observers as the dupes of surface appearances, the *ubiquity* of financial influences is undeniable, and it creates a problem for the expositor of the economics of finance.

The problem consists in the need to make the initial simplifying conceptions which are an essential part of the economist's tool-kit sufficiently comprehensive to bring out what are regarded as the main features of the part played by the monetary system in the operation of the whole economy. The (micro) price theorist can take a single market, set up his conceptual picture, and proceed quickly to the heart of his argument. The monetary theorist cannot avoid taking longer over the conceptual preliminaries, the effort to communicate to the reader his own (vastly simplified) picture of the economy and of money's place in it. Further, because of the divergences of view to which attention has been drawn it will be necessary in the course of the book to sketch the outlines of alternative pictures.

These conceptual preliminaries, then, are the concern of this introductory chapter, and the reader's indulgence and attention are requested. Act One may seem slow in setting the scene, but it is an essential build-up for the action to follow. What we are doing in this scene-setting is to arrange what are probably rather familiar ideas into the particular form required for the subsequent argument.

The circular flow of income and payments

We begin on what will certainly be, for many readers, familiar ground – the concept of the *circular flow of income*. We picture first a very simple closed economy without government, in which productive activity is organized by firms which buy productive services from the personal or household sector. These services are used to manufacture consumer goods which are sold to households, who purchase the goods with the incomes received from the sale of their services to firms. We further simplify, initially, by taking the stock of capital (both fixed capital equipment and inventories) as given and unchanging; and also by assuming that households spend the whole of their incomes, i.e. that expenditure E is equal to income Y. We then have a self-sustaining circular flow which can be visualized as Fig. 1:1.

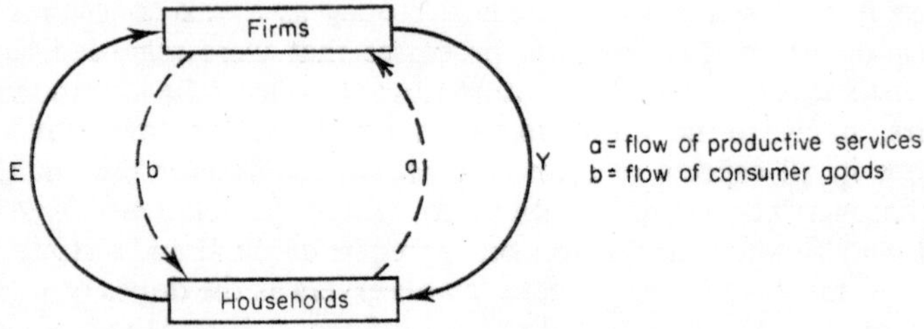

FIG. 1:1

It is now necessary to move a stage closer to reality by taking account of the facts that

(i) some part of households' income is likely to be saved, and saving (S) can be pictured as a *leakage* from the circular flow – part of their incomes which recipients choose not to spend, for the time being, on currently-produced goods, but to hold against the contingency of desire or need to spend in the future;

(ii) firms may wish to add to their stocks of capital equipment and inventories, i.e. to invest, and investment (I) can be pictured as an *injection* into the circular flow because it creates incomes for the suppliers of productive services used in the manufacture of the investment goods. (If we think for the time being of all saving being done by households and all investment by companies, it simplifies matters without affecting the underlying principles.)

Our flow diagram now requires some elaboration, as in Fig. 1:2.

Clearly the size of the circular flow, i.e. the level of the community's income per period of time, will be affected by the relationship between the size of the injection and the size of the leakage; for example, an excess of I over S will increase the flow – in real terms if previously unemployed productive services can now be drawn into employment, and in money terms (rising prices) if productive services were already fully employed. If $I = S$, the level of income will remain unchanged; but we have pictured decisions to save and decisions to invest as being taken in an unco-ordinated fashion by different groups, and there is no obvious reason why this balance should occur. Macroeconomic theories in the Keynesian tradition, however, lead to the ideas that

(i) *Ex post, S* and *I* in simple models are *necessarily* equal.
(ii) In the event of divergence between *S* and *I* in the 'planned' or *ex ante* sense, the level of income will change as a result of the multiplier process in such a way as to remove the divergence.

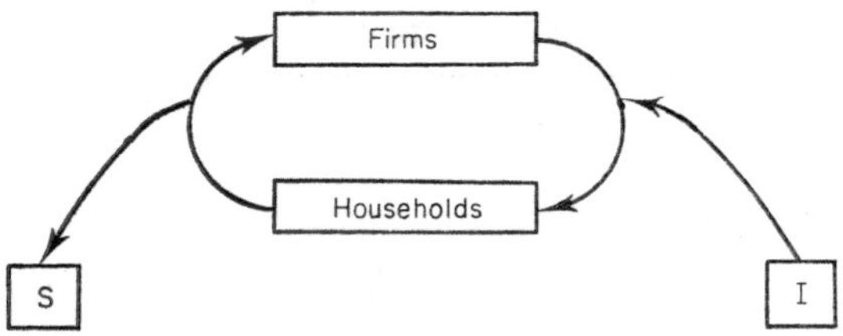

FIG. 1:2

(iii) Because the level of saving is closely dependent on the level of income whereas the investment level is not, the *direction of causation* is that represented by the arrows in Fig. 1:2. That is to say if we start from an equilibrium position, changes will typically occur because an 'exogenous' change in planned investment causes a change in income which causes the level of saving to change. It follows that, despite the *ex post* identity, we can say that the level of investment determines the level of saving rather than vice versa.

We shall take these arguments as given rather than following them through in detail. The main point that we need to bring out at this stage is that this approach, following the mainstream of early post-Keynesian thought, places exclusive emphasis on *one* channel of linkage between *I* and *S* although there are in fact *two* such channels. The emphasis so far has been entirely on the links running from *I* to *S* via the markets in *goods*, but clearly *I* and *S* are also linked through the *financial* markets. These markets are the major concern of this study, and we must now turn to building them into our elementary conceptual scheme.

The starting point here is the truism that investment expenditure must be financed. In practice of course, a good deal of the finance is provided from internal sources, notably from profits retained by firms instead of being distributed to shareholders. Our simplification (of assuming that all saving is done by the household sector) requires us to ignore such direct self-finance of investment; we concentrate attention on sources of *external* finance. In this connection, our basic picture is of firms borrowing funds on the 'capital market', these funds being provided by those who are refraining from spending the whole of their current incomes, i.e. by savers. (A fully consistent yet reasonably realistic theory, of course, would need by this stage to introduce carefully specified time lags, but our present concern is with fundamental insights rather than with rigour.) Savers may either lend direct to investing firms or may lend to financial institutions (e.g. banks, insurance companies) who in turn lend to 'ultimate' borrowers. So in Fig. 1:3 we now link *S* and *I* to form a 'capital circuit' separate from, though linked to, the 'income circuit' of Fig. 1:1.

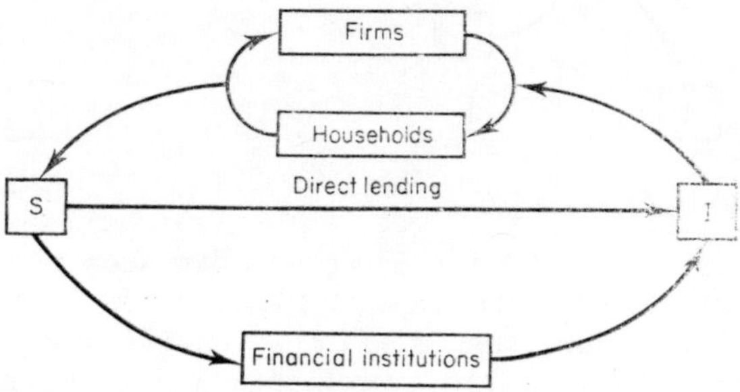

FIG. 1:3

Although Fig. 1:3 presents a rather more comprehensive and realistic picture of financial flows linking saving and investment, it should be noted that there is nothing in it that necessarily destroys the presumptions that the major *causal* links between *S* and *I* are the links via the goods markets, and that *I* has causal priority over *S*. So long as the causal chain $I \rightarrow Y \rightarrow S$ holds (i.e. so long as the level of *I* is not affected by the volume of *S*) then the capital market could be a purely passive intermediary channel through which borrowers undertaking real investment tap the sources of finance in effect created by the output- and income-expanding effects of their own investment. However, the extent to which capital market channels can properly be regarded as passive intermediaries in this sense is open to question. Full examination of this problem would require us to distinguish, among the financial institutions operating in the capital market, between banks and non-bank, or 'other', financial institutions – o.f.i.s, and to give extended consideration to each category.

The banks: money flows and money stocks

However, our focus of concern is on *monetary* management and accordingly we shall concentrate attention primarily on the first category, the banks, though we shall say something about o.f.i.s in Chapter 6. The main distinguishing characteristic of the banks is that their liabilities, in a highly developed economy such as that of the United Kingdom, comprise the major part of the economy's stock of money.

This statement immediately brings us face to face with one of the main conceptual difficulties in economics, particularly perhaps in financial economics. We are attempting to visualize financial *flows* through the economy, yet we are unable to avoid mention of financial *stock* concepts. It has become almost a cliché of theoretical exposition to observe that, at the level of formal logic, the distinction between flow theories and stock theories presents no problems because of the ease with which theories in either form can be translated into the other form. For example, if we have a theory suggesting that in certain circumstances certain economic units will desire to increase their stocks of a particular financial asset, then our theory clearly implies the existence of a desire for flows of that asset into the units' portfolios. But, as so often in economics, formal logic in this context does not take us very far, for reasons that will emerge shortly.

Returning, then, to the banks and their place in our conceptual scheme, we need to notice two (related) reasons for arguing that they have an importance beyond that suggested by regarding them as a passive channel through which funds flow from savers to provide finance for productive investment. Indeed, we shall see that it is possible to argue (although we shall in chapter 6 partly criticize and contest the argument) that the banks are largely *unable* to perform this intermediary function. As we are here approaching the heart of the debate concerning the nature and significance of banks' activities in aspects closely related to the techniques of monetary policy, we shall need to set out these two arguments rather carefully. The first argument concerns the (current) flow of bank credit or loans, and the second argument concerns the (accumulated) stock of bank credit.

Bank credit flows and credit creation

Stated baldly, the first argument is that the flow of bank credit is specially important because of the fact that banks can and do CREATE credit. That is to say, they can cause the volume of funds flowing into the finance of investment to exceed the volume currently being made available by savers lending their savings on the capital market. On this view, the banks might be regarded as playing an important (albeit conceivably still a passive) part in sustaining the Keynesian causal primacy of I over S as we have described it above. For, if we start from an equilibrium position in which $I = S$, and visualize the effects of a (permanent) rise in planned investment spending, it must be conceded that, however short the time lags might be, the process of $I \rightarrow Y \rightarrow S$ must occupy *some* time – so that there arises the problem of explaining how I is financed initially, until the multiplier process has generated an equivalent increase in planned saving.[1]

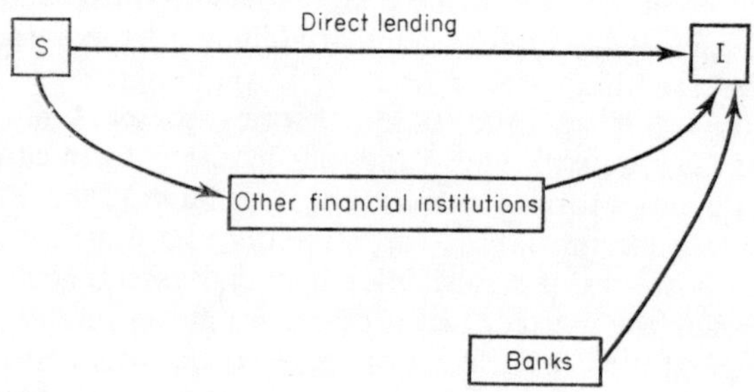

FIG. 1:4

If banks can create credit, however, then the strictly logical problem is solved, for the banks can in principle finance ΔI. We can now in Fig. 1:4 elaborate our scheme a stage further – omitting now, for simplicity, the circuit of 'real' expenditures and income generation. Clearly, however, we must, before passing on, explore the basis of the arguments for the view that banks possess the power to create credit, the power to lend purchasing power that has not previously been lent to them.

These arguments derive from the fact that it is the liabilities, the deposits, of the banks that actually circulate from one economic unit to another in the course of effecting the financial flows through the economy that we have been trying to visualize. Bank deposits, that is to say, form the main component of the medium of exchange in highly developed economies, dominating cash (coin and notes) in the performance of this exchange function. Were cash the only

[1] This important argument is developed later, in Chapter 6. It will be noted that the argument in the text abstracts from the categories of 'unplanned' I and S, by whose inclusion I and S can be presented (somewhat artificially) as necessarily equal in every period of time.

medium of exchange, we should have to think of banks as we might now think of, say, building societies—as borrowing exchange media from some and then re-lending to others that part of their borrowing that they did not need or desire to hold idle for reserve purposes; an increase in liabilities giving rise to an increase in assets.

The fact that bank deposits are themselves exchange media essentially reverses the sequence, it can be argued. We now think of a process in which the banks increase their assets (lend), and the concomitant rise in liabilities (deposits) circulates from hand to hand instead of being presented to the banks for exchange into cash. The notion of a *zero* cash leakage is, of course, over-rigid, but if we adopt it provisionally then we can set out the theory of the *bank credit multiplier* in its simplest form. We assume that the banks work to a conventional and rigid cash reserve to deposits ratio of x (say, 1:10). Then, following an accession of cash from whatever source, the cash ratio (with zero cash leakage) can *only* be restored by an expansion of bank loans and bank deposits that will be a multiple of the cash accession, the multiple being equal to the reciprocal of the cash ratio. Symbolically:

$$\Delta D = \frac{1}{x}\Delta C_b$$

where D = bank deposits, and C_b = bank cash. (Further, if the cash reserve ratio is fixed irrespective of the deposit total, so that the 'marginal cash ratio' = the 'average cash ratio', we can state the determinants of the total volume of deposits in similar terms:

$$D = \frac{1}{x}C_b).$$

It may be noted that we have here a concept that is logically a close analogue of the Keynesian investment multiplier mentioned above. There, a rise in investment (injection) caused an increase in income that continued until saving (leakage) balanced the initial injection. Here, a rise in bank cash (injection) causes an increase in bank deposits that continues until required bank cash reserves (leakage) absorb the initial injection. And just as one standard elementary criticism of the Keynesian investment multiplier is that it fails to take account of other leakages (e.g. to taxation and imports), so the simple bank credit multiplier can be criticized on similar grounds.

In particular, it is argued that there is need to take account of the likelihood, as deposits expand, of a leakage of cash into circulation. If we again take the simplest form of the argument by supposing that the public (like the banks) wishes to maintain an absolutely stable proportion between its cash holdings and its deposit holdings, then –

by a simple extension of the above argument that in no way undermines its essential basis – we arrive at an expression for the incremental bank credit multiplier of the form:

$$\Delta D = \frac{1}{x+y}\Delta C$$

where y = public's desired cash/deposit ratio, and C = total cash, whether held by banks or public. Further, if we now take account of the fact that the components of C (notes and coin) are liabilities of the monetary authorities, we arrive at the standard textbook proposition that the volume of bank deposits is easily susceptible of official control – the authorities are the source of cash, the cash not required by the public for small change is available to the banks as reserves, and the availability of reserve cash limits the ability of the banks to create credit and deposits.[1]

Returning to Fig. 1:4, we can tie these ideas into our evolving conceptual scheme by picturing an economy that is growing under the impetus of rising investment, perhaps in response to the profit- and corporate growth-maximizing behaviour of entrepreneurs, seeking competitive advantage by installing more advanced equipment, that has become possible due to technical progress. There is therefore a tendency of I to rise ahead of S, creating a demand for external finance that cannot be fully met from current saving. Let us assume (which is a great oversimplification, but we must needs proceed by stages) that 'created' bank loans are the only possible source from which the financing gap might be filled. Then the standard bank credit multiplier theory suggests that the extent to which the banks perform this service, and therefore the extent to which aggregate demand, output and incomes are permitted to grow, can be controlled by the authorities.

The details of the operation of this mechanism in a realistic institutional context will be explored in Chapters 2 and 3 where, as indicated in the Introduction, it will be argued that their simple

[1] Students are frequently confused or irritated by the fact that economists' explanations of the determinants of the quantity of 'output' (– loans and their deposit counterparts) produced by the banks make no explicit use of the microeconomic theories, based on profit maximization and/or other objectives, that are used to explain the determinants of output for non-financial firms. It might assist clear thinking if it is pointed out that it is quite possible to apply the standard theory of the firm to banks. Thus we can think of banks as seeking to attain the profit-maximizing 'output' at which marginal revenue equals marginal cost, but as constrained to a lower output level by the reserve ratio requirements to which they are subject. In this case it can be predicted that (until profit-maximizing output is attained) the banks will always respond to reserve increments by expanding loans and deposits and so moving towards the position they regard as optimal.

logic is a poor guide to real-world complexities. For the moment we continue the elaboration of the basic conceptual framework as we turn to the second argument against regarding banks as no more than passive intermediaries in the saving-investment process.

The stock of bank credit and the demand for money balances

This argument, as stated, concerns the *stock* of bank credit, and also is closely related to the foregoing discussion of the flow of bank credit. We have seen in the course of that discussion that the flow of lending by banks results in a by-product, as it were, of a stock of bank deposits. This fact, that a flow of bank lending to some economic units results in a stock of bank deposits that may in ultimate equilibrium be held by other economic units is one of the reasons why the distinction between the stock and the flow aspects of banks' behaviour is much more than merely a distinction between two forms of stating logically identical arguments.

What we are now concerned with, then, is the question of the relationship between the *demand* for bank deposits on the one hand, and on the other that *supply* of deposits which the standard theory sees as a by-product of bank lending. This question is of special relevance in the case of banks, it may be recalled, because in the case of o.f.i.s we think of the demand for o.f.i. liabilities coming first (in logical if not temporal sequence) and the flow of o.f.i. lending being constrained by changes in the public's willingness to hold the stock of o.f.i. liabilities. In the case of banks, the orthodox argument sees the sequence as being reversed, and we need to consider the process by which the demand for bank deposits adapts itself to changes in the supply.

The first (of two) points to be emphasized is that this *is* the situation implied by orthodox theory: the demand must adapt itself to the supply. Underlying the orthodox approach is the idea, initially perhaps rather strange, that the public cannot, except in very limited degree, influence the size of the stock of bank deposits. The basis of this idea can perhaps best be explained by considering the contrast between the possibilities open to a holder of (i) a building society deposit or (ii) a bank deposit. Taking (i), the holder can either retain the deposit or demand cash or a bank deposit in exchange for it – in the latter case the deposit is extinguished (and unless it can be replaced or reserves run down, the building society must call in loans to an equivalent amount). Turning to (ii), the alternatives open to the holder are retention or spending or lending. In the latter two cases, the deposit passes to other transactors who have the same alternatives.

This has been called, for sufficiently obvious reasons, the 'hot potato' theory of money: people can pass it around, but cannot consume (destroy) it. On the orthodox view, the notion needs to be qualified only by recalling that the public may change its desired ratio of cash to bank deposits; if the public withdraws cash, there will be a (multiplied) decline in deposits. But it can be argued that in highly developed economies, where the banking habit is already widespread and there is confidence in the banks' stability, significant shifts in the public's cash/deposit ratio are unlikely, i.e. that *y* in the equation on p. 00 will tend to be highly stable. The conclusion would be that the size of the bank deposit stock is almost exclusively determined on the supply side, and that with rigid reserve ratios the supply side influences are dominated by the authorities.

But – and this is the second point – even if it were true that the public collectively cannot influence the volume of bank deposits in existence, we need to remind ourselves again that individual economic units do not have to hold money balances against their will. Because bank deposits are generally acceptable exchange media, any deposits in excess of the desired level can be used to purchase either goods and services or financial assets. But if people are demanding additional goods, output and/or prices (real and/or money incomes) are rising; if people are buying additional financial assets, the prices of such assets are rising (interest rates falling). It follows that in an *equilibrium* situation (no excess supply of deposits) the whole stock of bank deposits must be *willingly* held.

Without necessarily committing ourselves to the precise Keynesian theory of the demand for money balances, we shall make considerable use in this book of the basic Keynesian framework within which this demand can be explained. This framework, it is well known, sees the demand for money as composed of two elements that are at least conceptually separable:

(i) There is a demand for 'active' balances, needed to satisfy the motives of providing for current payments, both those payments whose size and timing is predictable (transactions demand) and those whose size and timing are uncertain (precautionary demand). These balances may reasonably be assumed, it is argued, to vary pretty closely with the level of income and output, whose production and distribution they finance as they pass from hand to hand. These active (M_1) balances, then, must be thought of as circulating (provisionally, at a constant speed or velocity) through the income and capital circuits of Fig. 1:3.

(ii) There is also, however, a demand for 'idle' balances to satisfy the motive of providing protection against the possibility of capital losses should the prices of financial assets in transactors' wealth portfolios decline during the period for which the assets are held (speculative demand). These (M_2) balances, Keynes argued, would for two reasons tend to vary with the level of interest rates. First, the higher interest rates are the higher the income inducement to forgo the protection against capital losses offered by holding wealth in the form of money. Second, the higher interest rates are the more likely wealth-holders are to take the view that they will not, in the near future, rise further – so that the risk of capital losses recedes. Post-Keynesian writers have often tended to be critical of Keynes's speculative motive analysis of the demand to hold money as an asset; for example, because the market rate of interest will reflect the consensus of market expectations regarding future interest rates, and only rarely would some asset holders have such firm convictions as to be prepared to gamble that the market's expectations were wrong. Several alternative arguments have been adduced for the existence of an asset demand for money balances. For example, it has been argued that the precautionary motive can explain such a demand, because if the timing of payments is uncertain then the possession of money balances reduces the possibility of embarrassment and loss if an unexpected bunching of payments needs occur; but people's willingness to purchase this 'insurance' will tend to vary with its cost – the latter being represented by interest income forgone by holding money.

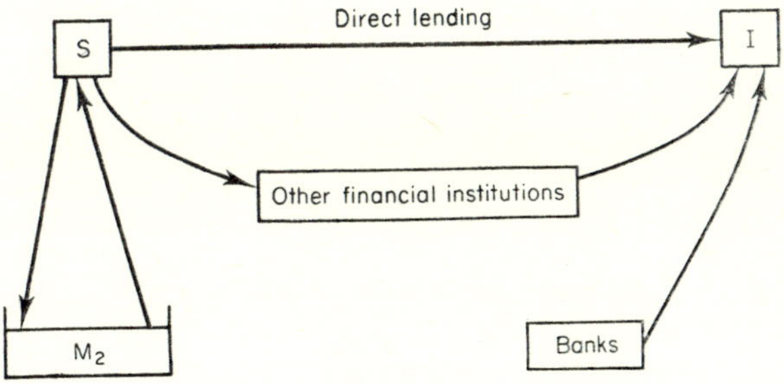

FIG. 1:5

By one route or another, then, we arrive at the notion of an asset or wealth demand for money that varies inversely with the level of interest rates. It has, too, been argued that a rise in interest rates might well stimulate efforts to economize on transactions balance needs by such means as the re-timing of transactions to achieve greater synchronization between money receipts and money payments. And we may comfort ourselves with the thought that, provided that any segment of the demand for money reveals any significant degree of interest elasticity, the essentials of the Keynesian approach are preserved. So we now need to elaborate the fund-flow scheme of Fig. 1:4 a stage further. In Fig. 1:5 we picture a reservoir of balances at least temporarily immobilized within the capital circuit. We may note in passing one reason why it was a 'great over-simplification' to think of new bank loans as the only possible source of finance for an excess of planned investment over planned saving; for, as the arrow leaving the M_2 tank reminds us, another source in principle arises from the activation of money balances previously held idle, i.e. an increase in the average velocity of circulation of total balances.

However, bank loans are for many borrowers the cheapest and most convenient source of finance, and we may probably assume that firms unable to tap current savings (or their own stock of M_2 balances) for the finance of investment would normally turn to this source if such loans are available – that is to say, within our present elementary and orthodox scheme, if the authorities are willing to create the necessary cash reserves to support a higher level of advances and deposits. Again referring back ,then, we can pick up the story of the operation of our flow model by visualizing the changes by which equilibrium is restored following a rise in planned investment financed by bank credit creation. What happens is that the increased stock (supply) of money becomes willingly held as a result of twofold increase in the demand for money:

(a) as real and/or money incomes increase, the required volume of active (M_1) balances rises. The size of the rise will depend on the income-velocity of circulation (Y/M), which we have provisionally assumed to be constant. Given the fact that Y will increase by a multiple of the original increment of I and M, it is theoretically possible that the required increment of transactions balances (ΔM_{1D}) will be larger than the increment of money stock (ΔM_S), in which case (since in the Keynesian scheme M_1 demand is assumed to have priority over M_2 demand) the stock of idle balances must be drawn down, causing a rise in interest rates as liquidity preference of wealth-holders is less fully satisfied. If for simplicity we suppose, however, that $\Delta M_S > M_{1D}$, then we can move on to

(b) that part of M not required for transactions purposes is absorbed into idle balances (enters the M_2 tank in Fig. 1:5) to the accompaniment of a fall in interest rates as liquidity preference is *more* fully satisfied.

Thus we begin to build up a mental picture of the way in which the stock and flow aspects of banks' operations might interact. The picture is unavoidably one of some complexity. It is essential to appreciate the flow aspects, because much debate on monetary processes and policy concentrates on them, to the confusion of students reared exclusively on stock models. For example, writers using the Keynesian model, with its emphasis on financial stocks, frequently expound the effects of an increase in bank credit extension in a way that, while in equilibrium it reaches the same ultimate result that we have done, reverses the temporal sequence in disequilibrium. These writers picture an increase in the stock of bank money being first absorbed entirely into M_2 balance holdings, to the accompaniment of a decline in interest rates. This latter decline is then seen as stimulating increased investment spending, and thus a (multiplied) rise in incomes which expands the requirement for M_1 balances so that some of the newly created, and initially idle, deposits are drawn into active use. It is true that this conceptual sequence can be defended as realistic if we visualize the new deposits arising from bank purchases of (government) bonds in the 'second-hand' bond market, rather than from bank lending for the direct finance of investment spending by the borrowers. In the former case, we picture bondholders surrendering bonds in exchange for bank deposits (rearranging their wealth portfolios) as interest rates fall (bond prices rise) in response to bank bond-buying. Thus the new deposits would indeed accrue initially to idle balance stocks, and we need for completeness to add an additional link to our flow scheme, as pictured in Fig. 1:6.

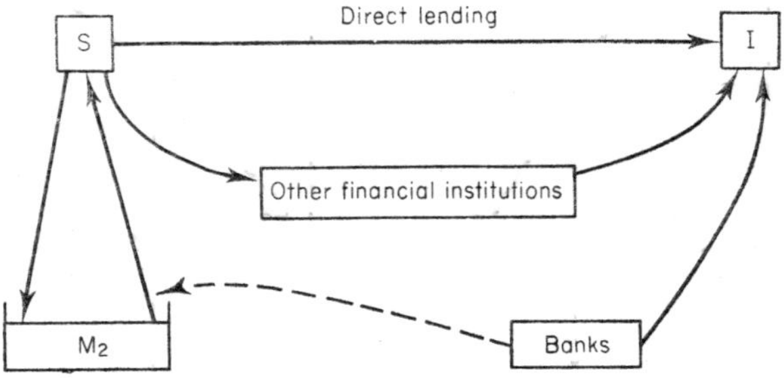

FIG. 1:6

This new link, it will be noted, breaks the neat and convenient one-way chain of flows of Fig. 1:5. It is certainly needed for completeness, and its existence emphasizes the complexity of the financial mechanisms with which we are wrestling. But the view here taken is that, if we are seeking a *realistic* conceptual scheme, we must regard this 'reverse flow' as an exception that proves the rule rather than as an exception that upsets the basis on which we have been arguing. For commercial banks of the type found in the UK tend to regard the making of advances as their prime concern, with their investments occupying a residual position among non-liquid assets. Therefore, when bank credit is expanded, we must think of the typical situation as one in which the bulk of the expansion takes the form of advances for the finance of investment spending. For this reason we draw the direct link between banks and our M_2 tank as a dotted line, reflecting a quantitatively weaker linkage.

The quadrant diagram of the Keynesian model

For such reasons, then, we retain our emphasis on the importance of the flow aspects of banks' activities, and for such reasons we have taken pains to build up the scheme of Fig. 1:6 which is developed further in Chapters 5 and 6 below. But as we have seen, the Keynesian model is more commonly visualized in ways that emphasize, on the financial side, the stock aspects. And there is in common use a stock diagram that is rather simpler because some of the detailed 'works' are hidden. Partly because of this simplicity and partly because of its familiarity, we shall find this diagram – or rather a section of it – extremely useful, and accordingly we set it out here in Fig. 1:7 – the well-known 'quadrant diagram' of the Keynesian system.

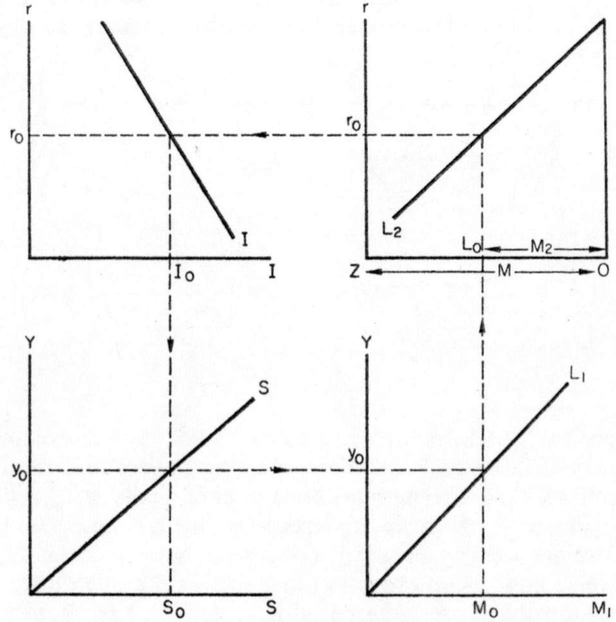

FIG. 1:7

Starting on the left-hand or 'real' side in the north-west quadrant, we have a schedule representing what Keynes called the marginal efficiency of capital, showing the level of investment varying inversely with the rate of interest as a result of the collective behaviour of profit-maximizing entrepreneurs. With a given interest rate r_0, therefore, we have the level of planned investment determined at I_0. In the south-west quadrant, we have a very simple savings function (NB that the scale on the vertical axis is relatively compressed) that shows the level of income (Y_0) which is an equilibrium level in the sense that it is associated with a level of planned saving S_0 that is equal to I_0.

Moving over now to the financial side, in the south-east quadrant we have the L_1 function that shows the level of active, money balances (M_0) required to finance the payments streams associated with income (Y_0). In the north-east quadrant (where the point of origin (O) is on the *right*-hand side and OZ measures the total stock of money in existence) we see that L_0 of money balances remain available to satisfy the asset demand for money summarized in the L_2 schedule. The latter schedule shows that L_0 of balances will be willingly held (i.e. equilibrium will exist in the money market) at the rate of interest r_0. So we have a simple summary of the interrelationships visualized in the Keynesian model between, on the one hand, the real flows of investment, saving and income and, on the other hand, the stocks of money supplied and demanded. It should not be too difficult to see that, making allowance for the shift of emphasis implied by casting the financial side of the model in stock rather than in flow terms – a shift some of whose implications we have already noted – Fig. 1:7 can be interpreted to tell much the same story as Fig. 1:6.

Bonds in the Keynesian model

We wish to note next, however, that these two diagrams also have in common what for our present purpose is a deficiency, namely that money is the only financial asset that is incorporated *explicitly*. We say explicitly, because the Keynesian model by implication includes non-monetary financial assets when it pictures wealth-holders choosing whether to hold their assets in the form of money or in the form of interest-bearing assets ('bonds'). We need to remember that the model refers essentially to a short period during which we can think of the total stock of wealth (both financial and real: we are concerned with the former but see p. **00** below) as being sufficiently stable for us to regard it as effectively fixed. It follows that, when our L_2 schedule shows that at high interest rates there is a small demand for money and vice versa, there is implied a 'bond-preference schedule' showing at high interest rates a large demand for bonds and vice versa. So we can expand the north-east quadrant of Fig. 1:7 to incorporate this bond-preference schedule (*B*) as shown in Fig. 1:8. (Readers who share the author's weakness for concrete visualization of arguments might now care to extend Fig. 1:6 by adding a 'bond tank' to the left of the M_2 tank, with an arrow from *S*. But it must be realized that, within our present rather orthodox framework of argument, there is a vital difference between the effects of flows into these two reservoirs. Flows into M_2 'break' the flow circuit because they represent savings that are not on-lent for the finance of investment. This is where we see the rationale of the argument that banks cannot act as intermediaries between saving and investment. Incomes are largely received in the form of the main medium of exchange, bank deposits, and a decision to save does not make additional lending resources available to the banks; if the savings are held in the form of idle deposits, then all we have is a decline in the velocity of circulation of bank deposits. By contrast, accumulations of stocks of bonds result – again as a sort of by-produce – from flows of savings that *are* lent to finance investment; in this case the decision to save need have no effect on the velocity of circulation.)

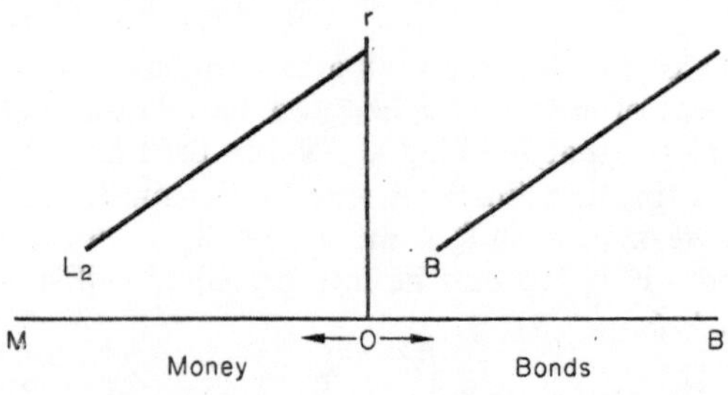

FIG. 1:8

Figure 1:8 shows only the demand schedules for financial asset stocks. The supply schedules can be pictured, provisionally, by simple extension of the standard arguments already described. Fig. 1:7 showed in effect a vertical supply schedule for money balances (i.e. a schedule completely inelastic to interest rates), reflecting the orthodox assumption that the size of the money stock is under the control of the monetary authorities and that the control normally operates in such a way as to reduce the volume of bank deposits below the level that would be reached in the absence of such control. But we must now realize that if, as at the present high level of abstraction, we have only one interest-bearing asset and therefore only one interest rate, the rate which produces equilibrium in the money market must also produce equilibrium in the bond market. It follows, therefore, that the authorities' supposed control of the money stock implies that the size of the bond stock in private sector hands is also under official control. Therefore we can also, provisionally, think of the effective bond supply schedule as completely inelastic. So, we have as a starting-point for our exploration of monetary management techniques the idea of the authorities determining the size of the money and bond stocks in the hands of asset-holders, these stocks in conjunction with asset-demand schedules determining the equilibrium asset price/interest rate, and this equilibrium interest rate being the main proximate *financial* influence on the level of investment spending and therefore on the levels of aggregate demand and output (income).

Volatility of 'static' schedules

It is desirable to emphasize the word 'financial' in the last sentence. As Keynes himself argued, and as modern investment theories such as the accelerator underline, the Keynesian marginal efficiency of capital schedule might well shift bodily, and frequently, under the impulse of other influences (income levels, expectations) on investment, apart from interest rate changes. That is to say, we are here attempting to use a very simple static model to interpret very complex dynamic developments as the economy moves through succeeding (short) time periods, and only at grave risk of oversimplification and faulty argument and conclusions could we attempt to press events slavishly into our simple framework. We do well, therefore, to realize at once that there might also be forces at work tending to cause our static financial asset-preference schedules to shift bodily, and that such shifts can (in a manner explored in some, but by no means exhaustive, detail in Chapters 2–6) greatly complicate the operations of monetary management. Of these forms, we will make preliminary mention at this stage of two possibly rather important types.

First, we should realize that – despite the simplification mentioned already – as savings are made from the income flows of successive time periods, the total wealth stock is in fact increasing. That is to say, there is a tendency for both our money and bond demand schedules to move outwards from the origin, reflecting willingness to hold asset stocks of increased size at any given level of interest rates. However, it is not by any means necessary that the schedules should move outwards at equal rates, i.e. that the *wealth*-elasticity of demand for money should be equal to the *wealth*-elasticity of demand for bonds.

Quantity Theory criticism of Keynes

Second, it can be argued that the Keynesian model oversimplifies in regarding interest income forgone as the only relevant cost of holding assets in the form of idle money balances. This view results from concentration on *financial* wealth, and thus on the money/income-yielding asset margin. But a more inclusive view of wealth-holding choices would take into account the fact that assets can be held in real rather than financial form, so that account would also need to be taken of the money/goods margin. In this latter context, the cost of holding money is represented by changes in the real value or purchasing power of money during the period for which the idle balances are held. Thus if a tranche of idle balances is held for a year, and if during this year the general price level rises by 5 per cent, then the effective cost of holding the money is the decline of 5 per cent in its power to command goods and services. Such considerations are the basis of charges by modern Quantity Theorists (who tend to emphasize the relevance of the financial asset/goods margin for wealth-holding choices) that the Keynesian money-preference schedule of Figs. 1 : 7 and 1 : 8 is based on 'money illusion' – confusion between the *nominal* value of money-holdings (M) and the *real* value (M/P), where P is the general price level. In consequence, it is argued that the Keynesian schedule, as specified by Keynes for a world of underemployment of resources and relatively stable prices, would tend to be unstable in a world of full or near-full employment and inflationary tendencies. For an increase in (nominal) M, contrived or permitted by the central bank, might indeed reduce interest rates temporarily as predicted by the Keynesian model. But the expansionary demand tendencies caused by, or accompanying, the rise in M and reduction in r would also intitiate or strengthen inflationary tendencies. A rise in prices to a level expected to persist would tend to move the Keynesian money-preference schedule outwards from the origin if asset-holders wished to preserve a given stock of monetary purchasing power in real terms (thus tending also to restore r to its original level). While a rise in prices that stimulated very strong expectations of further increases in the future would tend to move the Keynesian schedule inwards towards the origin. The general implication is that it is more fruitful to think of money supply money demand and interest rates in real rather than in nominal terms. We shall return to consider briefly this line of argument when we examine and criticize the relevance of recent Quantity Theory-type models in Chapter 7.

For the moment, we are content to notice that, even within the confines of this rather exploratory discussion of influences on the demand for money, we have grounds for thinking of this demand as subject to a rather complex array of influences. We have mentioned the level of income, the level of wealth, the level of interest rates and expectations of future interest rates, the level of prices and expectations of future price movements. Even in a stable environment with rather steady expectations, it would clearly be quite a problem to quantify these influences separately so as to provide a clear picture of the demand situation in the financial markets in which the monetary authorities operate. When we have a fast-changing environment, with inherently volatile expectations, the difficulties are compounded, and we see the force of Professor G. L. S. Shackle's reference[1] to Keynes's bravery in attempting to write 'earthquake economics in a static equilibrium framework'. Though we shall, of necessity, use the static framework extensively, we could ignore the tendency to seismic tremors only at our peril.

Strengths of the Keynesian framework

Before passing on to the meat of this study, however, we shall complete our preliminary survey of concepts and tools by noticing one respect in which the Keynesian framework is *more* useful than might at first sight appear. This arises from the fact that the model's usefulness is not closely dependent on the specific form of the relationships envisaged, but rather it can be regarded as a sort of shorthand summary of a general type of approach to analysing financial influences on aggregate demand. In particular, we can advance the following two propositions.

First, while the formal Keynesian model sees 'the rate of interest' as the major linkage between financial markets and goods markets, it is not in fact dependent on any notion of perfection of asset markets with the associated idea that the price/yield of assets is the only variable stimulating supply and restricting demand. The Keynesian approach can be quite easily adapted to take account of: (a) the existence of many sub-markets dealing in claims of different types and maturities, and giving rise to a structure of interest rates rather than a single rate; and (b) the fact that in many of these sub-markets demand for funds (= supply of assets) is accommodated to a limited supply of funds (= demand for assets) by means of varying degrees of credit rationing rather than entirely by interest rate changes. Thus in effect we can regard 'the rate of interest' as a shorthand term for the whole complex of conditions on which capital markets make finance available to different types of borrowers. Provided only that when liquidity preference becomes more/less fully satisfied, this complex of conditions tends to become less/more

[1] *Economical Journal*, June 1961.

restrictive of borrowing, the Keynesian simplification does not lead to faulty reasoning.

Secondly, while the Keynesian model thinks of investment, and by implication concentrates on fixed investment, as the expenditure category that might in principle be sensitive to changing financial conditions, it can be adapted to situations in which other categories, such as inventory investment or purchases of consumer durable goods, are envisaged as responsive to such changes.

Future programme

In the next two chapters we shall use the simple Keynesian apparatus summarized in Fig. 1:8 as a starting-point for critical examination of the techniques by which the monetary authorities might in principle exercise an influence on the level of aggregate demand by their operations in financial markets, and for evaluation of the practicability of such influence in an institutional setting whose complexity contrasts strongly with the simplicity of the analytical apparatus. We shall concentrate discussion on the use of methods of influence/control that work through market mechanisms, as opposed to methods that rely on directives to financial institutions – though the latter will be mentioned in Chapter 7. As already implied, such market controls can be sub-divided into *price* and *quantity* aspects; in our present context, that is, into aspects primarily concerned with on the one hand the cost (and/or availability) of credit, and on the other hand the quantity of bank deposits. Because it raises more complex questions, and because it has been increasingly prominent in recent debate, we shall give more direct attention to the quantity aspect. And because deflationary policies have dominated the scene in recent decades, we shall analyse the means by which the bank deposit stock might be *reduced*; it would be more realistic to discuss the possibilities of enforcing a reduction in the rate of growth of deposits, but this would complicate the argument without much changing its essentials.

While we shall in Chapters 2–4 be following convention by discussing control of the *stock* of bank deposits, it must again be emphasized that neglect of the flow aspects emphasized in this present chapter is admissable only as a preliminary simplification. Reference to Fig. 1:6 makes clear that reduction in the money stock can in principle be accomplished

either by inducing the public to run down its holdings of M_2 balances by exchanging them for bonds previously held in the asset portfolios of the banks;

or by effecting a reduction in bank advances that would constitute a 'negative flow' of finance for investment spending (or, of course, by some combination of the two).

In the former case, the tendency for interest rates to rise might' along Keynesian lines, affect the levels of investment, income and savings. In the latter case, investment might again fall, because of reduced availability of finance, or alternatively the reduction of bank finance might (as the Radcliffe Committee argued) be offset by increased borrowing through other channels at some increase in cost. In either case there would, then, be disturbances to supply and/or demand conditions in the money and other financial markets – disturbances that are apt to be overlooked unless the financial flow aspects are brought out explicitly. We shall return to these flow aspects in Chapter 5.

Monetary and fiscal policy

In both Chapters 2–4 and Chapter 5 we shall be concerned with the problem of policy-induced deposit reduction, but in two different contexts that are frequently not adequately distinguished by commentators on current policy. In Chapters 2–4 we shall be concerned with what might be called the 'monetary policy' case; in Chapter 5 we turn to the 'fiscal policy' case.

The importance of the distinction can perhaps best be seen by noticing that in the fiscal case we need to analyse the effects of overall government policy under two headings:

(i) decisions about the size of the budget surplus/deficit have *direct* implications for the level of income that are frequently analysed in a Keynesian framework by using the concept of 'budget multipliers'; an increased surplus represents a net reduction in the autonomous expenditures that constitute the basis of the income multiplier, and an increased deficit represents a net injection into the income stream;

(ii) in addition, however, decisions concerning the method of finance of a budget deficit, or the use made of a budget surplus, affect the financial situation with possible *indirect* repercussions on the levels of expenditure income.

In the monetary policy case, however, all the decisions fall into category (ii), i.e. they can only affect the level of income indirectly, via the financial situation.

A possibly more concise and relevant way of making the distinction is to say that in the fiscal case income, savings and wealth are all changing (assuming policy's aims are realized) *as the direct result of current government policy decisions*, so that government's actions affect the demand for financial assets as well as the supply. By contrast, in the monetary case the central bank can be thought of as taking the budget position along with private sector spending propensities as given, so that total wealth and the demand schedules for financial assets are also given, and policy action is directed at influencing the maturity distribution of the given total of financial assets.

We can simplify, in effect, then, by thinking of the 'wealth changing' and the 'wealth given' cases. Both because of the latter's relative simplicity and because of its greater relevance to problems of monetary management and policy *per se*, we shall begin with it and treat it at greater length; its rather complex and interlocking aspects will occupy us in Chapters 2–4.

CHAPTER 2

Monetary Policy: Short-term Asset Markets

We begin our discussion of deflationary monetary policy with the highly abstract model pictured in Fig. 1:8. Absurdly simple as this model may seem as a representation of the bewildering complexity of financial markets, it contains all the essential elements of the ideas that most economists have in mind when prescribing the techniques by which such a policy can be carried into effect by a central bank. Reference to the diagram (reproduced, with small modifications in Fig. 2:1) will make immediately clear that, if the central bank wishes to 'tighten' financial markets, it simply sells bonds from its own portfolio to the public. As these bonds are purchased, the public runs down its money balances, so that the bond stock in the hands of the non-bank public rises, and the money stock falls, to the accompaniment of a fall in bond prices (= a rise in bond yields). The bank credit multiplier theory implies that the central bank will not need to sell bonds to the full extent of the desired reduction in M, but only to the extent necessary to produce contraction of bank cash on a scale that will induce the banks themselves to reduce loans and thus deposits.

The central bank's open-market operations can, on this view, be regarded as having potent effects on M by virtue of the 'leverage' inherent in the bank credit multiplier process. But, as the diagram again makes clear, there is one substantial limitation on the central bank's power; if it sets the level of M, it must accept the interest rate level (r) at which the financial markets will be in equilibrium. The converse holds, of course, if the central bank makes r its 'target variable'. So we have the standard proposition that the central bank can control M or r, but not both. This proposition is widely accepted as a factual statement, but we shall argue that it is very probably an over simple conclusion based on what is certainly an over simple model.

However, before we move, as this last statement implies is necessary, to a lower level of abstraction, we can use our abstract picture to bring out two basic questions that need constantly to be remembered if we are to avoid losing our way in institutional detail.

The first question concerns the (price) *elasticity* of our asset-preference schedules. As the extreme situations visualized in Fig. 2:1 show, much depends on the degree of elasticity. If the schedules are highly inelastic (Fig. 2:1a), influence on r will be easy, but it will be difficult for the central bank to exert much control over the level of M; and conversely for elastic schedules (Fig. 2:1b). In the intermediate case of elasticities in the region of unity, the central bank can exert substantial influences on both r and M, though of course it cannot *in the short period* make both variables move in the same direction. (The short period reference here needs emphasis, because of the fact that, over the cycle, M and r tend to move up and down together in boom and recession, a phenomenon that might be provisionally and simply explained by supposing that in the upswing the need for liquidity expands to a greater extent than the supply, and vice versa. This situation does, however, create complications for debate on monetary measures, because Keynesians emphasizing interest rate policy tend to regard the cyclical movement in interest rates as evidence that the authorities are following correct anticyclical policies, while Quantity Theorists tend to draw opposite conclusions from the cyclical movement of money stock.)

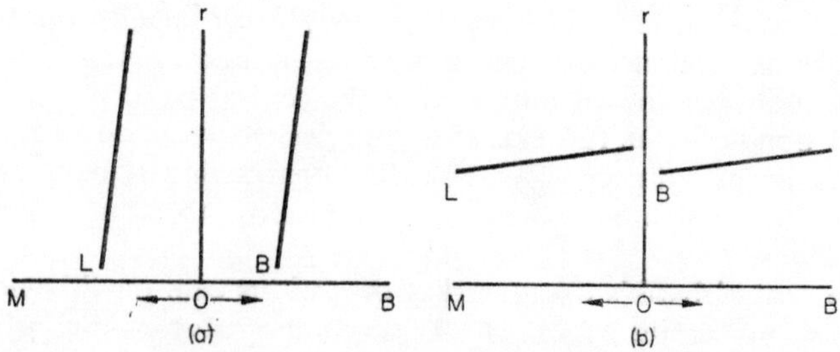

FIG. 2:1

This matter of elasticities is one to which much attention has been devoted in recent years by econometricians. By contrast, our second basic question has usually been played down by academic writers, though it tends to receive much emphasis from practitioners (as it did from Keynes himself); it concerns the *stability* of the asset-preference schedules. The sort of problem that would be posed by instability is perhaps obvious enough, but it can be pictured in terms of Fig. 2:2. Suppose that with schedules L and B, the authorities attempt to reduce the money stock from M_0 to M_2 by pushing the interest rate up to r_1. They will be frustrated in this objective if, either as *effect* or *accompaniment* of their open market operations, the schedules shift to L^1 and B^1, in which situation r_1 must for equilibrium be accompanied by a larger money stock (M_2) instead of a smaller one. Of course, money stock M_1 could in theory still be attained at an even higher interest rate, but the attempt to raise r further might have additional complications of types we shall explore at a later stage.

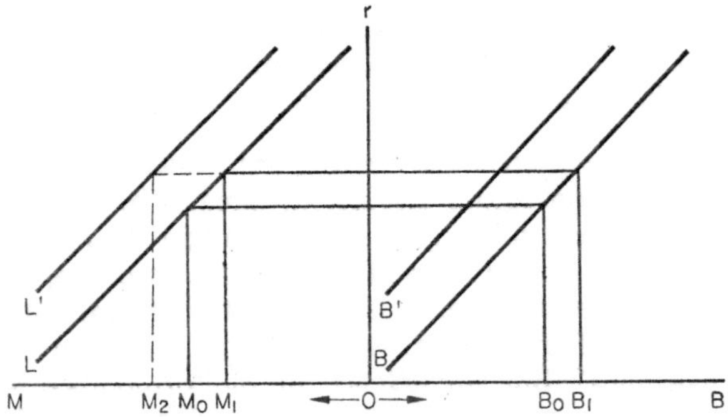

FIG. 2:2

With these basic questions in mind, we now proceed to a more detailed analysis of the techniques of (deflationary) monetary control in a rather more realistic setting. The institutional background we shall have in mind is, naturally, that of the United Kingdom; but because readers might wish to have some basis on which to judge the extent to which our conclusions are dependent on, or independent of, the particular features of this background that are in greater or lesser degree unique to the UK, an appendix to this chapter contains a brief discussion of monetary policy under different types of institutional arrangements.

So we concentrate here on the UK, and in order to facilitate readers' admission to what has become a rather voluminous and slightly esoteric literature, we shall begin with a brief historical survey of the English debate. The central question of the discussion can be summed up as:

> Can the authorities effectively use the leverage provided by the (clearing) banks' cash ratio to produce a desired change in the volume of (clearing) bank deposits?

The English debate on monetary control

There have been long periods in recent decades when this has seemed to be one of the least controversial questions of monetary theory. In 1931, for example; the report of the Macmillan Committee (para. 222) crisply summarized accepted views that we shall here describe as 'old orthodoxy':

'. . . in making an adequately high bill rate effective in the market, the Bank of England varies the amount of its assets, and hence of its deposits, to the necessary extent, which, in turn, has the effect of changing on a much larger scale the quantity of credit made available by the joint stock [clearing] banks, since, when the banks' deposits at the Bank of England are increased by a given amount, these banks feel themselves free to increase their own assets by nine or ten times this amount.'

It is hoped that the reader faced with this statement will, in the light of the foregoing conceptual discussion, already be asking himself some pertinent questions – e.g. what effect might the increased flow of bank loans have on the flows of expenditure, income and savings, and thus on the size of the wealth stock and the demand for financial and other assets (Fig. 1:6)? How stable and elastic are the asset demand schedules? But, in defence of old orthodoxy, we must emphasize that the great bulk of academic debate has shared its dependence on partial equilibrium analysis and its concentration on the supply side of the market in monetary assets. This restriction of the scope of the argument is basically due to acceptance of the view that the private sector cannot influence the level of M but can only adapt itself to a money stock exogenously determined. In reviewing the debate we shall need often to follow the restricted view, but we shall return to the broader picture in due course.

In the mid-1950s an alternative to the Macmillan approach was formulated, and quickly commanded sufficiently widespread acceptance aptly to be called a 'new orthodoxy'; this approach, in one form or another, stressed the crucial role in modern conditions of the banks' liquid assets ratio rather than of their cash ratio. More recently, there have been several attacks on new orthodoxy from a standpoint sufficiently close to the position stated in the Macmillan report that we may label it neo- [old] orthodox.

In order that the relationship between these various doctrines can be clearly appreciated, we shall make a preliminary attempt, using what has been well described as a 'five-finger exercise', to clarify the range of logical possibilities stemming from restrictive open-market operations by the central bank. For this purpose we shall use a highly stylized model of the UK system that enables us to abstract from the many institutional changes of recent decades.

Logical arguments

Table I sets out hypothetical balance sheets for the London clearing banks and the discount market respectively. (In the table, figures that have changed from the previous *relevant column* are in italics; note that columns 4a and 4b are alternatives – described below – to follow column 3.) It is assumed that the banks are working

TABLE I. *London clearing and discount market (hypothetical balance sheets)*

London Clearing Banks £m	(1)	(2)	(3)	(4a)	(4b)	(5)		(1)	(2)	(3)	(4a)	(4b)	(5)
Deposits	10,000	*9,950*	9,950	*9,904*	*9,904*	*9,375*	Cash	800	*750*	*796*	*750*	*750*	750
							Call money	750	750	*704*	704	704	704
							Bills	1,350	1,350	1,350	1,350	1,350	*1,200*
							Other assets	7,100	7,100	7,100	7,100	7,100	*6,721*
	10,000	*9,950*	9,950	*9,904*	*9,904*	*9,375*		10,000	*9,950*	9,950	*9,904*	*9,904*	*9,375*
							Cash ratio, %	8·0	7·5	8·0	7·6	7·6	8·0
							Liquid assets ratio, %	29·0	28·6	28·6	28·3	28·3	28·3

Discount Market £m	(1)	(2)	(3)	(4a)	(4b)	(5)		(1)	(2)	(3)	(4a)	(4b)	(5)
Call money from L.C.B.	750	750	*704*	704	704	(4a) or (4b) re-peated	Bills	600	600	600	600	*554*	(4a) or (4b) re-peated
Other	250	250	250	*296*	250		Bonds	400	400	400	400	400	
Loans from B/E	—	—	*46*	—	—								
	1,000	1,000	1,000	1,000	954			1,000	1,000	1,000	1,000	954	

to an 8 per cent cash ratio, and that the cash is held entirely in the form of bankers' deposits at the Bank of England. The liquid assets ratio is initially at 29 per cent; the minimum level is 28 per cent. (The budget and the balance of payments are both assumed to be in overall balance, so that the total Exchequer debt is stable; the implications of relaxing these assumptions will be noted in due course.)

Column 1 represents an assumed initial equilibrium position, in which the cash ratio is at 8 per cent. Column 2 shows the impact of an open-market sale by the authorities of £50 million of securities (the type of security sold does not greatly matter for the present, but we can conveniently think of bills) to non-bank holders. This sale will, of course, tend to be accompanied by some upward pressure on interest rates, but we concentrate for the present on the impact effect on the banks' balance sheets. This effect is a reduction of both bank deposits and bank cash by £50 million, so that the cash ratio declines below 8 per cent. (In the Bank of England's balance sheet, the Banking Department's bills and bankers' deposits both decline by £50 million, but this is not an essential part of our story and is omitted for simplicity.)

As is customary, the banks are assumed to restore their cash ratios by withdrawing call money from the discount market. Column 3 shows the effect of the withdrawal of the £46 million required to restore the 8 per cent cash ratio at the now lower level of deposits. The discount market replaces the lost call money by borrowing £46 million from the Bank of England, pledging bills as security for the loan.

We now come to the first significant item in our catalogue of logical possibilities. As lender of last resort, the Bank of England does not refuse requests from the discount market for loans to enable the houses' books to be balanced. It can, however, choose to lend either (A) at prevailing market rates, or (B) at a higher rate that is penal, in the sense that it will involve the market in losses, since it exceeds the running yields on bill portfolios.

Provided that the banks are not worried by the slight reduction in their liquid assets ratio, the first possibility brings the sequence to an end with the situation depicted in column 3. To the accompaniment of a (probably mild) increase in short-term interest rates, bank deposits have fallen by the amount of the official open-market sales, and that is that. The analysis of the second possibility, however, involves us in speculating on the efforts that it may be supposed the discount market will make to escape from a disequilibrium position. Again, there would seem to be two possibilities. The houses might try to eliminate the penal borrowing either (1) by replacing it with funds borrowed from sources other than the clearing and central banks, or (2) by reducing their (bill) portfolios.

The effects of the first alternative are illustrated in column 4a of Table I. It is there assumed (realistically) that no significant private sector bodies other than the clearing banks maintain accounts at the Bank of England. It follows that what the discount market borrowed would, in fact, be clearing bank deposits. The use of these deposits to repay loans from the central bank would thus involve a further reduction in both the deposits and the cash of the clearing banks. The cash ratio would again fall below the minimum acceptable level. If the discount market were to choose the second alternative, however, the effect on the clearing banks' cash ratio would be the same. This is shown in column 4b. We can envisage that the market fails to replace £46 million of bills as they mature, and uses the proceeds (clearing bank deposits) of the maturing bills to repay the loan from the Bank of England.

Either way, therefore, the banks again find themselves with an unacceptable cash deficiency. They might be supposed to react by further withdrawals of call money from the discount market, repeating stages 3 and 4, with a further reduction of their deposit totals. But it must be noted that their liquid asset ratio is already close to the 28 per cent minimum, and the result would be to reduce it below this level.

Thus, the banks have reached a point where adjustment of their cash (and liquidity) ratios can be achieved only by reducing their higher-yielding assets: investments and/or advances. Neglecting for the time being all complications of the kind hinted at in the paragraph in parenthesis on page **00**, a possible final equilibrium position is shown in column 5. Bank deposits have declined by £625 million to £9,375 million; £625 million is equal to 12½ or 100/8 times the initial cash reduction of £50 million. The liquid assets ratio has declined close to the 28 per cent. minimum, the banks – like, probably, the discount market – having run down their bill portfolios.

Let us consider this decline in the bill holdings of the banking system (defined to include the discount market as well as the clearing banks). Logically, the decline might result from one or other of two factors: (i) net sales of bills to non-bank holders, which could happen regardless of whether or not the total *supply* of bills changed; (ii) a reduction in the total volume of bills outstanding, which could be effective even had the banks' *demand* for bills remained unchanged. And – final taxonomic distinction – sales of bills to non-bank holders might occur; either (a) at the initiative of the banking system in offering less for bills and selling bills at lower prices, or (b) as a direct response of the non-bank public to the higher return on bills resulting from official action, in selling bills on the open market and/or raising Bank Rate. The implications of this last distinction may not be entirely clear, but should become so in the course of the exposition.

We may summarize the outcome of our five-finger exercise in the following way. Action by the central bank to reduce the quantity of bank credit produces its first *impact* on bank deposits and on the cash position of the banking system. The consequent disturbance of the cash ratio, and the banking system's reactions to this disturbance, imply the catalogue of logical possibilities regarding *secondary* effects shown in Table II. Thus (A) gives the result that bank deposits fall by the amount of the central bank's open market sales. (B), in any one or combination of its variant forms, gives the result that bank deposits fall by a multiple of this amount, the size of the multiplier being given by the reciprocal of the cash ratio.

The *logic* of the foregoing arguments is not open to challenge. All we have done is to elaborate on a basic proposition of banking theory – that if the banks work to a rigid cash ratio and if the central bank is able and willing permanently to reduce the quantity of cash available to the banking system on terms acceptable to the system, then somehow or other bank credit and bank deposits must be reduced to restore the ratio of deposits to whatever quantity of cash is available on acceptable terms. The *empirical relevance* of the arguments depends on the way real-world institutions work, or could be made to work. The doctrines we are about to review stand or fall on the question of whether their statements concerning

TABLE II. *Central bank alternatives*

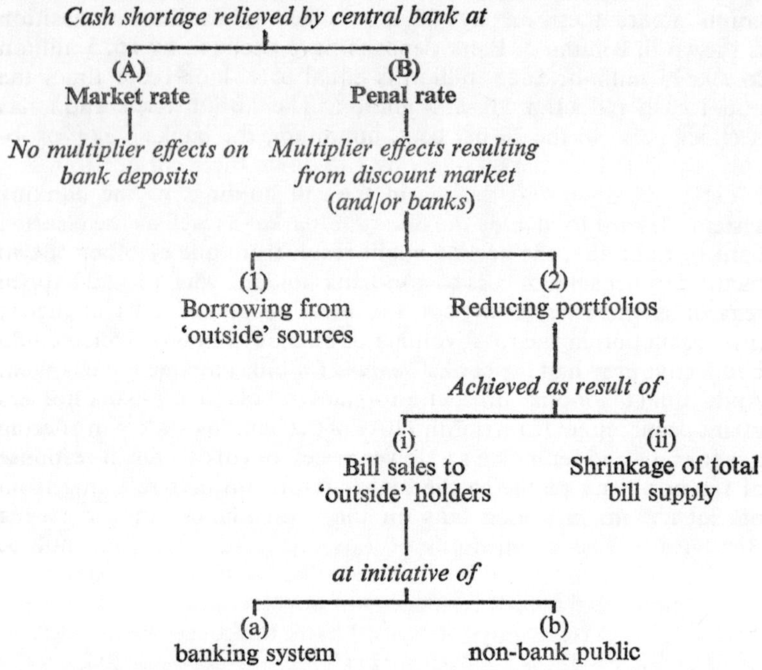

institutional realities are correct – or have been correct, for institutional workings change through time.

Empirical arguments

In terms of our schema above, old orthodoxy of the kind typified by the quotation from the Macmillan report rested its case for the empirical validity of the bank credit multiplier theory primarily on possibility (B) (2) (ii) of Table II. The effect of restrictive open-market policy on short-term interest rates was stressed, as was the effect of an increase in short-term interest rates in reducing the total volume of commercial bills of exchange outstanding. Table I can thus be interpreted in these old orthodox terms by emphasizing the commercial, as opposed to the Treasury, element in the 'bills' category of the banks' and discount houses' balance sheets; by visualizing column 4b rather than column 4a as following on column 3; and by regarding the reductions in bill holdings shown in columns 4b and 5 as primarily the outcome of a decline in the demand for bill credit (= supply of bills). This is, perhaps, the main reason why old orthodoxy ignored any complications from liquid assets on the central bank's ability to operate on the banks' cash position; restrictive policy was thought to have the effect of reducing the available supply of liquid assets.

The enduring empirical validity of this notion is doubtful. It does not take account of the possibility of the banks gaining a larger proportion of a reduced supply of bills. In any case, would this supply in fact decline? Later work has tended to weaken economists' confidence in the interest-elasticity of demand for credit (at least until rates rise to such high levels that they produce other complications). It is possible that in the heyday of 'the bill on London' a rise in UK short-term interest rates worked in the desired direction, because arbitrage caused bills seeking discount to be deflected to other international centres. But in gold standard conditions there was a possible offset in that inward 'hot money' flows would tend to replenish the banks' cash reserves (cf. Chapter 4 below). These archaeological matters need not detain us, however, because we shall see in Chapter 4 that international flows operate very differently in the current UK institutional setting.

In the mid-1950s, however, observers perceived another reason for questioning the relevance of old orthodoxy, viz. the rise to dominance of the Treasury Bill in banking system bill portfolios. Longer perspective suggests that this dominance may only have been temporary, as the figures in Table III suggest.

TABLE III. *London clearing banks (averages of monthly figures, £ millions)*

	1952	*1960*	*1968*
Total liquid assets	2,097	2,299	3,182
of which Treasury Bills	950	1,007	468
commercial bills	105	142	527

But whatever future developments may bring, we now notice that one of the two main forms of *new* orthodoxy – we can call this form 'Model 1' – resulted from the perception that ascendancy in the 1950s of the Treasury Bill removed the *possibility* that the system could operate on strict old orthodox lines. Manning Dacey and W. T. C. King explored the implications of the fact that, in one of D. H. Robertson's memory-catching phrases, 'the unoffchokable Treasury [had] displaced the offchokable trader as the predominant drawer of bills of exchange'. Whatever may have been or been true of the demand for commercial bill finance, no one has yet argued that the demand for short-term credit by Her Majesty's Treasury is sensitive to fluctuations in short-term interest rates.

Thus, in formulating new orthodox Model 1, Dacey and King argued that (B) (2) (ii) no longer operated as a channel by which the effects of cash stringency were transmitted through the banks' asset structures until total bank credit and bank deposits had responded in the theoretically appropriate fashion. They were, of course, aware that (B) (2) (i) – bill sales to non-bank holders – was formally an obvious alternative. For reasons that will become plain, but which our roughly chronological account of the debate requires us to delay examining, they concentrated here on alternative (b) – sales at the initiative of the public rather than of the banking system. Like many other commentators at the time, they were impressed by evidence that 'outside' (domestic) demand for Treasury Bills had increased substantially during some years of the early 1950s. This change was widely interpreted as being a reaction to the widening gap between Treasury Bill rate and the deposit account rates offered by the clearing banks; in this sense the change was at the initiative of the public.

In spite of this recent experience, the formulators of Model 1 did not regard (B) (2) (i) (b) as a reliable vehicle of the bank credit multiplier process, and this perhaps for two main reasons. First, it was open to the banks, official surveillance permitting, to retaliate by raising deposit rates in relation to Bank Rate to neutralize the competitive advantage of Treasury Bills. Second, if a really effective squeeze on bank credit and bank deposits took hold, it was probable that outside holders of Treasury Bills would liquidate their holdings on a significant scale to finance expenditure, and the supply of Bills to the banking system could increase rather than decrease.

Overall, therefore, in new orthodox Model 1 possibility (B) (2) as a whole was largely discounted. Because, at that stage, the discount market did not borrow on a significant scale from any source other than the central and clearing banks, (B) (1) was not yet operationally relevant. The conclusion was clear. A cash shortage engineered by open-market operations had to be relieved initially by the central bank in its capacity as lender of last resort. Even when this relief was provided at penal rates, however, no reliable mechanism was in operation that would enforce a multiplier contraction process on the banks – so long as the banks possessed 'excess' liquid assets that could be used to force the authorities to recreate the lost cash.

It followed that there was little point in vigorous use of the penal rate mechanism for the purpose of controlling bank deposits. And this brings us to new orthodox Model 2, which emphasized the implications of the central bank supplying cash at non-penalty rates, and which can now be described very briefly. For we have already seen that if the central bank, from free choice or *faute de mieux*, relieves a cash shortage at market rate – possibility (A) in Table II – the cash-base multiplier process cannot operate. This Model 2 is more closely associated with the writings of the third acknowledged founder of new orthodoxy, Professor R. S. Sayers, and is embodied in the report of the Radcliffe Committee issued in 1959 (cf. para. 376).

Again, however, it must be noted that this neutralization of the effects of open-market operations on the cash-base depended on the banks possessing liquid assets in excess of minimum requirements. From this followed the main practical conclusion, shared by both new orthodox models, that control of bank deposits could still be achieved if the authorities could influence the total of the banks' liquid assets.

Such influence could, in principle, come about in two ways: by official sales to the non-bank public of, respectively, short-term or long-term debt. Given that, for reasons some of which have already been mentioned, it was regarded as undesirable to concentrate effort on providing the private sector with large quantities of marketable short-term claims on the public sector, the prescription was that the authorities should attempt to sell enough long-term bonds outside the banks to facilitate the required reduction in the floating debt and, hopefully, the banks' liquid assets. That is, control of bank liquidity was to be achieved by the technique of funding the national debt. Any reduction in liquid asset totals so produced would, given that the banks were fairly close to the minimum liquid assets ratio at the start of the process, tend to produce a multiplier reduction in bank deposits something over three times as large as the initial liquid asset reduction.

It will be seen that the new orthodox prescription implied the assumption of a close link between the size of the floating Exchequer debt and the size of the clearing banks' liquid assets. This linkage rested on two implicit propositions; first, that a change in the size of the floating debt would tend to be reflected in a change in the banking system's Treasury Bill holdings would tend to cause a similar change in bank liquid asset totals.

Both of these propositions were necessary for the empirical validity of new orthodoxy, and a glance at Chart 1 below is enough to explain this doctrine's formulation during the 1950s and its decline during the 1960s. The substantial 'gap' in the latter decade between Treasury Bills and liquid asset totals has been filled by expansion in the categories of commercial bills (cf. Table III), and call money to discount market and other borrowers.

In face of this decline of new orthodoxy, attempts have been made to adapt the Macmillan-type approach to the modern institutional

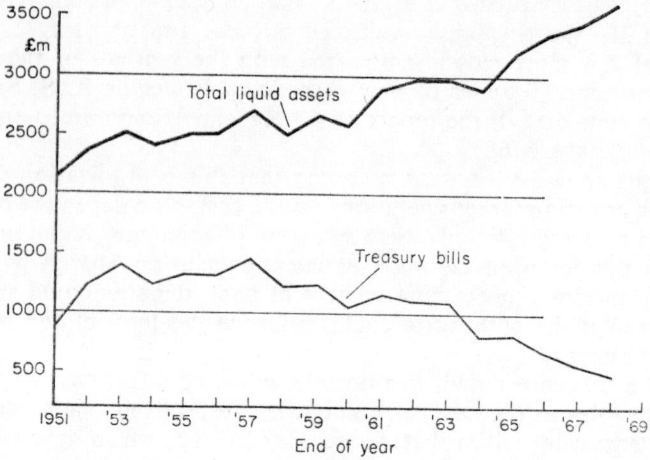

CHART 1

setting, and this brings us to neo-orthodoxy – which, as the brand of orthodoxy recently most prominent in UK literature, we shall examine in some detail. It might, however, assist readers in keeping track of the somewhat involved argument of this Chapter if we recapitulate briefly before embarking on this examination.

In attempting to assess the power of the central bank to bring about a reduction in the stock of bank deposits by making open-market sales of securities, we have:

(i) argued that the basic requirement is that the private sector's security preference schedules should be sufficiently elastic and sufficiently stable;
(ii) reviewed the *logical* variants of the basic bank credit multiplier argument that suggests that the central bank's power to achieve control of bank deposits is adequate;
(iii) cast doubt on the present-day *empirical* validity of several of these variants.

So, we now return to neo-orthodoxy as the most recent attempt to defend the orthodox bank credit multiplier theory in the UK institutional setting.

We have seen that the banks can (in the absence of direct controls) increase their liquid asset totals in spite of official pressure on these totals via reductions in the volume of Treasury Bills available for bank portfolios. The question relevant to the main topic of this chapter, however, is whether the banking system can in current conditions *contract* its liquid assets at will, and whether such contraction would facilitate reduction of the volume of bank deposits.

The neo-orthodox (cf. e.g. W. T. Newlyn, *Economic Journal*, June 1964) argue or imply that, in face of a cash stringency brought about by open-market operations and relieved only at a penal rate, the discount market (and at a later stage the banks themselves) will – contrary to the new orthodox position sketched above – both wish to reduce their liquid asset totals and be able to do so. That is, they are stressing item (B) (2) (i) (a) in Table II above. In terms of Table I they are conceiving column 4b as a stage of the multiplier process and thinking of the discount market, at its own initiative, taking up fewer bills (or selling more bills).

(Some neo-orthodox writers have also stressed possibility (B) (1) in Table II and column 4a of Table I. They envisage the multiplier contraction of bank deposits being facilitated by the discount market refinancing its portfolio from cheaper sources as an alternative to reducing security holdings. This possibility, which, as we noted, arises from post-new orthodox developments in financial markets, will be discussed in Chapter 4.)

Argument for possibility (B) (2) (i) (a), given the total volume of Treasury Bills issued, must be based on the view that the non-bank demand for bills can be represented by a stable curve showing larger amounts being demanded at higher discount rates (lower prices). It would follow that, if the discount market raises the rate at which it bids, more bills will be taken up outside the market.

Analytical tools

In order that the full ramification of this deceptively simple-looking argument can be made plain, we shall return to our diagrammatic apparatus – which now needs, however, to be elaborated slightly. We shall take out of the 'bond preference schedule' of Figs. 2:1 and 2:2 a (Treasury) bill preference schedule, leaving the bond schedule to represent all interest-bearing financial assets other than bills. This gives us Fig. 2:3. We continue to draw the left-hand segment with x axis reversed as a reminder that the L schedule is 'torn out' of the full Keynesian model as set out in the version of the quadrant diagram in Fig. 1:7. The curved arrows in Fig. 2:3 are explained below.

For the time being, we concentrate on the Treasury Bill market, and elaborate slightly our picture of it, in the direction of realism (Fig. 2:4). Given the convention in the UK system that the discount market 'covers the tender', i.e. bids for all the bills on offer, we can picture the preference curve *TB* becoming infinitely elastic at the

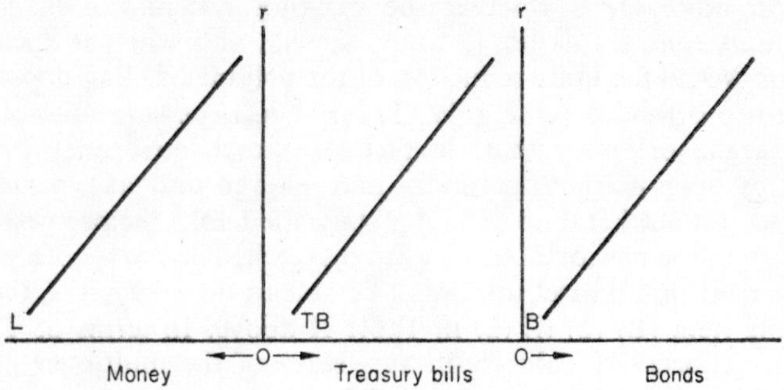

FIG. 2:3

discount market bid rate – which for simplicity we assume to be equal to the market's reserve rate, below which it will not sell bills from its existing portfolio. On the supply side, we recall that Treasury Bills play a residual role in financing the public sector. It follows that the total volume of bills in existence is equal to that sector's accumulated stock of liabilities held outside the public sector minus that part of the stock that the rest of the economy is willing (with the given conjuncture of interest rates, expectations and so on) to hold in the form of long-term debt. Accordingly we picture the supply of bills *TBs* as being absolutely inelastic to interest rates, although *TBs* may well move bodily from week to week as the Exchequer's residual financing needs change and the quantity of newly issued Bills diverges from the quantity of maturing Bills.

We can now restate the neo-orthodox argument. In the initial position, with equilibrium rate r_0, 'outside' holdings are *OA* and

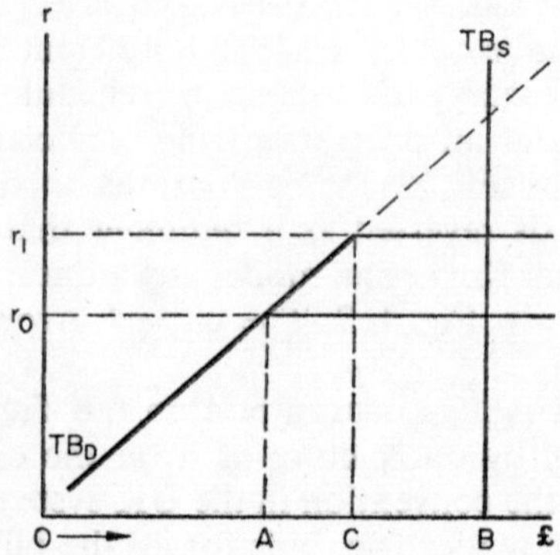

FIG. 2:4

discount market holdings *AB*. When the market raises its rate to r_1, outside holdings expand by *AC* as the market's holdings fall to *CB*. So, the squeeze on bank cash resulting from the central bank's open-market security sales is envisaged to be transmitted to reduced liquid asset holdings by the banking system as a stage in the multiple reduction in the system's assets and liabilities (deposits).

Nothing, apparently, could be simpler and more probable. Yet a moment's reflection suggests that the argument is incomplete until we have asked *where the funds AC diverted into the Treasury Bill market come from* and what further repercussions there might be. Reference back to Fig. 2:3 makes clear that, leaving aside the possibility of a purchase by the central bank that would of course undo the effects of the original open-market sale of securities, there are two main possibilities; these are shown by the curved arrows. The purchase of *AC* of bills by outside holders might in principle be financed

(a) by running down holdings of money balances; or
(b) by sale of some other interest-bearing asset.

The question of the relative likelihood of these two possibilities has large implications for the neo-orthodox argument. We shall examine each in turn, and argue that (b) is in fact much the more probable.

Taking (a) first, we shall glance in turn at analytical and empirical considerations. On the analytical side, we may remind ourselves that any reduction in the stock of money must fall *either* on that part of the stock that has been held idle as in the standard Keynesian model *or* on that part that has been in active use, circulating from one holder to another in making loans and settling debts. (Such a precise division between 'active' and 'idle' balances is, of course, impossible in practice; the distinction is thus of conceptual rather than operational usefulness.) Active balances can be reduced in one of two ways: either by reducing expenditure – a Quantity Theory-type idea on which we shall comment in Chapter 7; or by economizing on the need for active balances in the manner mentioned earlier – an extension of Keynesian ideas.

There are thus plenty of theoretical reasons for backing (a), whose importance to neo-orthodox theory is that it would enable a policy-induced credit multiplier reduction of bank deposits to proceed. This reduction would be accompanied by reduced spending if the Quantity Theory approach were valid, or if the Keynesian *MEC* schedule (Fig. 1:7) were elastic to interest rates. If the Quantity Theory approach is not valid, or if the *MEC* schedule is totally inelastic, spending would not decline. Either way, the public is 'adapting itself to a money stock determined exogenously.'

A realistic analysis

But when we turn to empirical considerations, we encounter an immediate snag. For we have to realize that the institutional operators in 'wholesale' short-term asset markets like the Treasury Bill market do not hold idle balances on any significant scale, nor are they active large-scale spending units. Therefore none of the theoretical tendencies noted above are likely in this case to be of much *direct*, immediate practical relevance. It is true that it can be argued that operators other than financial institutions, notably large industrial companies, might be induced by a sustained rise in short rates to search for means of compressing their need for active balances, but this sort of development takes time and only relatively quick reactions are of relevance in the present context. This is one of those points in the argument at which we perceive the limitations of abstract models like that in Fig. 1:7, however useful such models may be in setting out the general framework of argument. It must be emphasized that we shall still not be describing what economic theorists rather quaintly call 'the real world', but for a conception of the situation in terms that even begins to approach realism, we must turn to possibility (b).

We wish to analyse the case, then, in which a rise in the yield on Treasury Bills *relative to yields on other assets* causes some holders of such assets to change the composition of their portfolios by switching into bills. The italicized phrase is important, however, and it raises issues that require some preliminary exploration.

We need now to recognize a severe limitation on the usefulness of our diagrammatic scheme as set out in Fig. 2:3. This scheme was originally based on the standard Keynesian model, containing one interest-bearing asset ('bonds') and, therefore, only one interest rate. A change in this single interest rate is conceived as causing, with given schedules and given total wealth, a change in the relative proportions in which asset-holders wish to hold money and bonds. It should be clear that, in attempting to apply this model directly to a situation with more than one interest-bearing asset, we should implicitly be assuming that all asset yields/prices move together without any time lag. Not only would this be unrealistic, but also it would plainly be inadequate for analysis of the sequence described in the previous paragraph.

It follows that to proceed with the analysis we need a new curve that relates the market's (stock) demand for Treasury Bills to its own yield, as opposed to the general level of asset yields. That is to say, we need a schedule showing, in principle, what would happen to the market's preference for Treasury Bills if the yield on other assets remained constant in addition to the schedule of Fig. 2:3 which shows what happens to the preference for bills when all asset yields change together.

Empirical estimation of *ex ante* demand schedules is always difficult because the only data we ever have is *ex post*. But at the conceptual, qualitative level our present problem is of easy solution, because we can have resort to a standard proposition of elementary demand theory, viz.,

> the demand for a particular brand of a commodity is more elastic than the demand for the commodity itself.

To take a simple example, the (flow) demand for *X*'s cigarettes D_x, will be more elastic than the (flow) demand for cigarettes as a whole D_c, because if the price of *X* cigarettes alone moves, some smokers will switch between *X* and other brands. This is shown in Fig. 2:5.

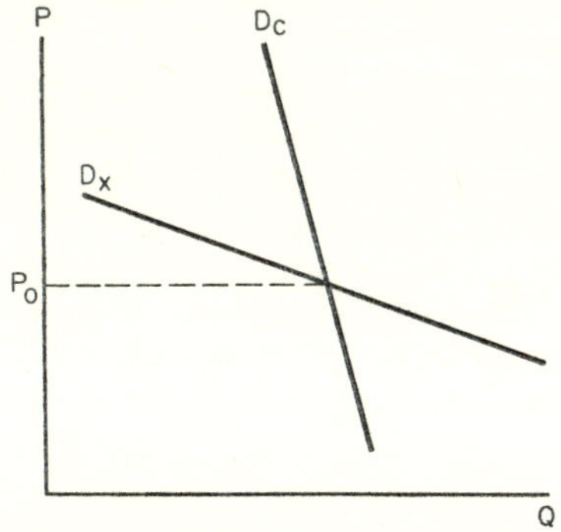

FIG. 2:5

For our present purposes, then, we want a (stock) demand schedule for Treasury Bills that will probably be rather elastic, and also a similar schedule for the asset from which transactors may be supposed to switch. In the UK institutional context, this latter might reasonably be thought of as short-term loans to local authorities (the market in which is often called the market in 'temporary money'); but it should be emphasized again that we are dealing in general, though basically realistic, principles rather than analysing an actual situation at a point of time – market situations and practices change, but our basic argument should remain valid for other than really major changes.

So we are now attempting to picture the interaction of two markets in which the 'goods' are very close substitutes for each other. That is to say, where D = demand, r = yield, and the subscripts b

and 1 refer to Treasury Bills and temporary money respectively, we have:

(1) $TB = (f)r_b, r_1$
(TB varies inversely with r_b, positively with r_1), and
(2) $LA = (f)r_1, r_b$

Diagrammatically, we can picture the two markets as in Fig. 2:6. Note that the demand curves are both represented as being highly price-elastic, reflecting the presumed high degree of substitutability of the assets and the consequent high cross-elasticity of demand between the two markets. We now *ignore the discount market* for simplicity, and treat the *AC* of bills of which the market is seeking to divest itself (Fig. 2:4) as effectively an increase in the supply of bills to outside holders, so that the supply schedule shifts from TB_s to TB_s^1. Note that the supply schedules (= demand for loans, in the accumulated stock sense, be it remembered) are drawn completely inelastic to interest rates. This expresses in perhaps rather extreme form a reasonably realistic assumption: that, in the short period, a given total of short-term Exchequer and local authority debt must all be held by someone. A sufficient rise in short rates would tend of course to stimulate refinancing by the issue of long-term securities, but we shall in any case argue (in Chapter 3) that this would complicate the argument without necessarily much changing its conclusions; therefore, provisionally, we adopt the simple assumption of total inelasticity.

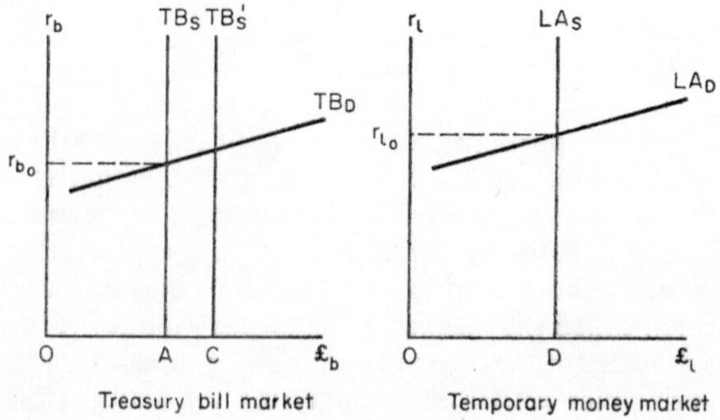

FIG. 2:6

The effect of this assumption on the operation of our model is rather startling. It is *to remove the possibility of equilibrium being restored* following the disturbance envisaged. We begin from the equilibrium position r_{bo}, r_{1o} (Fig. 2:6), with r_{1o} slightly higher on account of local authority securities being marginally less attractive than Treasury Bills; and we examine the sequence following an increase in the supply of Treasury Bills measured by *AC*.

This sequence is illustrated in Fig. 2:7. The steps are:

(i) a rise in the Treasury Bill yield to r_{b_1}, causing *AC* of funds to leave the temporary money market;

(ii) at r_{1_0}, there is therefore a decline of $YZ = AC$ in the demand for local authority securities – that is to say we have a leftward shift (not necessarily of equal size throughout the whole length, but drawn so for simplicity) in the whole demand curve, which now shifts to $LA_D{}^1$, passing through *Y*;

(iii) the concomitant rise in the local authority yield to r_{1_1}, restores the original differential between yields in the two markets, so that with relative preferences unchanged $AC = YZ$ would be re-attracted from the Treasury Bill market to the temporary money market;

(iv) at r_{b_1}, therefore, there is now a demand deficiency that causes the Treasury Bill demand schedule to shift to $TB_D{}^1$, and the yield to r_{b2}.

And so on and so on. What we get is a spiral of rate increases that goes on indefinitely without restoring equilibrium. But on reflection this is not really surprising, because what we have envisaged is an entirely closed system with the total supply of securities $= OC+OD$, a total demand for securities $= OA+OD$, and $OC>OA$.

Exception has sometimes been taken to this argument and its conclusions, on the ground that a rise in yields is accompanied by a

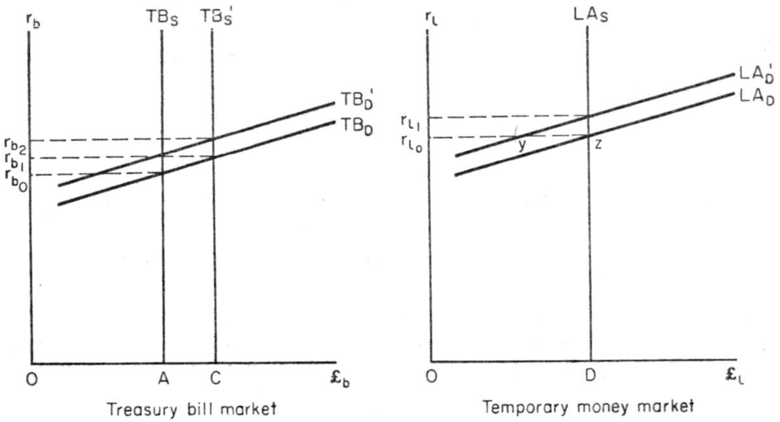

FIG. 2:7

fall in prices. Accordingly, if we take 'the total supply of securities' as being given by the physical quantity denoted Q, multiplied by the price per 'security' denoted P, then as prices fall $P \times Q$ declines and total supply is thus accommodated to the total demand for securities (= supply of funds). This is valid if we take a momentary or extremely short period view of the market, in which period Q can be taken as absolutely fixed. In fact, however, from day to day and from week to week borrowers' total needs for funds are changing, and in any case old securities mature and so existing borrowings need to be refinanced. So, there is a need on the part of borrowers for a certain *volume* of fund inflows, $P \times Q$. It follows that a decline in P as yields rose would need to be matched by an increase in Q. It is for this reason that the x axes in Figs. 2:4, 2:6 and 2:7 have been labelled '£' ($= P \times Q$) rather than 'Q'. In the local authority market, in any case, borrowings are not secured on negotiable instruments of fixed redemption value, and Q has no realistic meaning. In the Treasury Bill market borrowings *are* so secured, and Q has some purely formal significance; the authorities do offer for sale each week a certain *quantity* of bills each representing claims to £x thousand at a specified future date. It follows that the volume of funds $P \times Q$ raised at each tender cannot be known precisely in advance, because P is not precisely known. The potential difficulty here is overcome by a process (which also has other objectives) in which the Bank of England normally offers for sale more than enough Bills to cover the Exchequer's estimated needs, with a view to creating a 'tightness' which the Bank can relieve by buying Bills back from the market during the ensuing week. In practice, then, the effect of P falling below the Bank's forecast would be simply to create rather less 'tightness' than planned and so result in rather fewer repurchases than would otherwise have been made. (The details of the process are very clearly described in the article 'The Management of Money Day by Day' in the Bank of England's *Quarterly Bulletin*, February 1963.)

Conclusions

We have admitted that the entirely closed two-market system assumed in the foregoing exposition rests on rather extreme assumptions that will need to be relaxed before we can be satisfied that we have a reasonably realistic working model in mind. But we have also argued that the basic principles of this model are themselves reasonably realistic, and before passing on we shall look at two of their practical implications.

First, we notice that at stage (iii) of the sequence set out above, the discount market, as residual holder of Treasury Bills by virtue of its agreement to 'cover the tender', would be required to reabsorb the *AC* of bills of which it was supposed originally to have divested itself. That is to say, it is a corollary of our approach that (contrary to neo-orthodox assumptions) the discount market will have little control over the size of its bill portfolio. Two kinds of evidence can be adduced in support of the view that this is in fact the case. On the one hand, this interpretation has been widely accepted by close students of the way the market has actually functioned; witness, for example, Dacey and King's neglect of possibility (B) (2) (1) (a) in Table II. On the other hand, statistics of the weekly Treasury Bill tender show that, when the discount market reduced its bid price compared with the previous week, the percentage of Bills allotted to it is rather more likely to rise than to fall and especially so during periods of generally restrictive monetary policy.

Second, the tendency for interest rates to move up and down more or less in step with one another, a further corollary of our approach that can also be supported by observation of events, is capable of inhibiting the central bank from severely squeezing the cash-base – at least in the absence of supporting direct controls. The inhibition arises, *inter alia*, from the possible adverse effects of a strong and fast upward rate spiral on institutions whose rate structure is 'sticky'. A practical example can be derived from experience in the United States in 1966, when the savings and loan associations (roughly equivalent to UK building societies) were seriously embarrassed by deposit withdrawal stimulated by intense competition for deposits from squeezed banks. The Federal Reserve system (the US central bank) was obliged to relax the squeeze for fear of provoking payments stoppages by illiquid savings and loan associations and the consequent threat to confidence in the entire credit structure. In the more recent squeeze of 1968/9 the Federal Reserve avoided this embarrassment by using direct controls to prevent the banks from highly competitive bidding for small and medium deposits.

However, if the central bank has to use direct controls to restrict the money supply, that in itself is partial refutation of doctrines based on the bank credit multiplier approach, which imply that supposedly superior market weapons are capable of producing the desired result. We shall have more to say on this whole theme (cf. Chapter 7) but for the moment we simply notice one very basic principle that has emerged from our discussion. The central bank has the twin duties of *supporting* financial markets, and of *controlling* these markets in the interests of general macroeconomic policy. These duties can in certain circumstances conflict, and in the absence of some reconciling expedient the central bank must give priority to its supporting role. This point needs to be stressed as being of central importance. Academic discussion of monetary management in general, and orthodox bank credit multiplier theory in particular, have in recent decades almost totally neglected consideration of the support duty; it is our argument that this neglect has resulted in false conclusions concerning the potency of monetary policy in (consistently) controlling the money stock.

We must now move the argument on a stage further. For, so far, we have concentrated attention almost entirely on the short-term markets. But the long-term public sector securities market must obviously be brought into the picture. For the central bank can make open-market sales that increase the effective *supply* of securities in this market; the supply might also increase if the situation of stalemate and rising rates in short markets induced, say, local authorities to fund debt. Or, alternatively or additionally, the short market stalemate situation might be relieved by a process of switching from long markets that reduced effective *demand* for long-term securities. (It will be noted that we have given here two reasons for conceding that the earlier assumption of a closed system in short markets was over simple, but that the repercussions in long markets imply the creation of disequilibria there.) In Chapter 3 we shall examine the implications of such considerations in our quest for enlightenment on the potentialities of restrictive monetary policy.

APPENDIX TO CHAPTER 2

The Institutional Setting and Monetary Policy

As noted earlier, the banking system of the United Kingdom (like other aspects of the country's social/economic institutions, such as the trade union movement) exhibits certain peculiarities that lack exact parallels in other countries. This is of course to be expected, for a country's institutions are fashioned by complex influences arising from historical circumstances, national character and ideology, the influence of particularly powerful personalities, and so on. But these peculiarities, though adding immeasurably to the interest and fascination of a world that would be dull indeed without them, create difficulties for the student of social arrangements. It is taxing enough to master the essential features of one (constantly if slowly changing) set of institutions. Having done so, more or less, the question arises of the extent to which ideas based on this mastery can be carried over to the corresponding institutions of other countries.

So, the student of the UK banking system, having with greater or lesser effort familiarized himself with the functions of the discount houses, the mysteries of the Treasury Bill tender, the significance of the banks' liquid assets ratio and so on, faces a further barrier to understanding when he reads press reports of, say, a new Federal Reserve Bank ruling under Regulation Q; or of a variation in banks' reserve requirements against sight liabilities to foreigners imposed by the Deutsche Bundesbank. Such barriers are not easily surmounted after a lifetime of study, and no more than a modicum of progress can be expected from brief discussion here. But some progress is better than none. We shall argue that beneath the surface diversity there is a good deal of uniformity of basic principles. The author's belief (and it should be stressed that it cannot be more than a belief based on judgment from limited knowledge) is that this uniformity is sufficient to render the discussion of this book relevant to the operation of monetary policy in all advanced economies rather than to the UK only. One example in support of this belief has already been cited, and further supporting argument will be given from time to time.

Let us break into the problem by mentioning some aspects of what we have called the surface diversity. To do this we shall take some characteristics of the UK system (with which we assume readers to be familiar), and give examples of contrasting arrangements in the United States—though later we shall extend the argument. In selecting contrasts for mention, we shall concentrate on aspects more rather than less directly relevant to the operation of monetary policy.

One contrast that is often a source of difficulty for students can be disposed of quite quickly. The London discount market has no exact parallel in New York. The latter centre does have specialist dealers in government securities who fulfil some of the functions of discount houses, but the functions of these dealers do *not* include the traditional discount market role of acting as a 'buffer' between the central and the commercial banks. Thus, there is no equivalent in New York of the London convention (in any case weakened in recent decades) that the commercial banks do not have direct dealings – in particular do not borrow from – the central bank. But this contrast does not materially affect the mechanisms of monetary policy, as the Radcliffe report emphasized (para. 180). One can imagine that the discount houses were absorbed by clearing banks, that the balance sheets of the two sectors were thus amalgamated, and that the clearing banks dealt regularly, instead of only intermittently, with the Bank of England. Given that the clearing banks observed the same conventions and practices as the discount houses, in particular that they took over the commitment to cover the Treasury Bill tender, all could proceed much as now. If this view is valid, the analysis of central bank policy actions in Chapter 2 in no way depends for its validity on the discount market's existence and buffer role.

Because, as we saw in Chapter 2, official efforts in the UK to influence the banking situation for policy purposes have relied on the existence of certain conventions with regard to ratios of particular classes of asset (cash, liquid assets) to total assets, we can usefully narrow the field of attention down further by concentrating on the assets side of the balance sheets of the major commerical banks. We shall have reason later to draw attention to UK/US contrasts related more closely to the liabilities side, when we discuss the question of competition for deposits between banks and other financial institutions (cf. Chapter 6).

Turning, then, to the commercial banks' reserve assets, we can begin by looking at the practices of banks in the two countries, and we immediately come up against an obvious major contrast. In the UK, we have seen, the clearing banks adhere with more or less complete rigidity day by day to the 8 per cent cash reserve ratio (observance of which is now virtually a matter of compulsion, because it is the subject of a 'request' by the Bank of England that could be transmuted in case of need into a directive, under powers granted by the Act that nationalized the Bank in 1946). This degree of rigidity indeed dates back only to 1946. Before that, the clearing banks held 'excess reserves' of varying size – as the American commercial banks still do.

The general theoretical significance of banks holding variable excess reserves is easily seen. If we were to adopt the framework of the orthodox bank credit multiplier theory, then clearly changes in the actual reserve ratio observed by the banks would cause corresponding alterations in the size of the multiplier coefficient. It would follow that changes in the size of the reserve base, whether brought about by central bank action or by other forces, would no longer have precisely predictable effects on the banks' loan and deposit totals. For example, the banks might react to central bank open-market policy that caused the absolute volume of their reserves to shrink, not by calling in loans and so reducing deposit totals, but by allowing their reserve ratios to fall, leaving loan and deposit totals unchanged. The possible extent of such reactions is of course limited by the banks' need to ensure that the ratio does not fall below the *minimum* level imposed by convention or by central bank precept. None the less, the existence of excess reserves in itself creates the possibility of an extra degree of 'slippage' between central bank action to change the size of the reserve base and any effects on the macroeconomic aggregates that the central bank is seeking to influence. Recognition of this problem was one reason for the Bank of England's 1946 request that the practice of the clearing banks' holding excess reserves should be brought to an end.

However, even at the level of theoretical principle, the matter is more complex than our discussion so far implies. From the standpoint of the commerical banks' ability to wriggle out of the intended effects of central bank pressure on their reserve base, there are at least two additional factors that require mention – one tending to increase the banks' ability to wriggle, and the other to decrease it. In respect of both factors, there are contrasts between the UK and US systems, at least on the surface.

The factor favourable to the banks' powers to frustrate the intended effects of monetary policy is the possibility of tapping some reserve source other than the central bank: as we have seen, the orthodox theory of banking rests heavily on the notion of the central bank being the dominant, if not the exclusive, source of commercial bank reserves. The logic underlying the theory is clear. If, when the central bank squeezed those types of bank reserves within its own sphere of influence, the banks could acquire other reserves from some alternative source, then the squeeze could be rendered ineffective.

Today, the English clearing banks have no such alternative source of *cash* reserves, with the sole and in the short period relatively unimportant exception that in theory they could – by offering improved interest rates or better services – entice the public to acquire additional bank deposits by surrendering 'cash in the pocket'. Around the turn of the century, however, there was much discussion of the possibility that the clearers might hold gold stocks independently of the Bank of England, and had this practice developed the Bank would have faced difficulties in influencing the banks' loans and deposits through pressure on the cash base.

In the sphere of *liquid* assets as opposed to cash reserves, we have seen that the clearing banks have been able to create such assets (e.g. commercial bills of exchange) by their own lending practices, but the decline of the new orthodox theory that stressed the importance of the liquid assets ratio means that this aspect is relatively peripheral to our enquiry, and need not detain us.

Turning to the US, however, we find that the commercial banks have been less completely dependent on the Federal Reserve system for reserves, not because they can acquire elsewhere reserves as such, but because of their ability to acquire deposits to which the normal minimum reserve regulations do not apply. This ability arises from the existence of the large-scale Eurodollar market, a market in deposits denominated in dollars organized by banks in London and other financial centres. The American banks have offices in these centres, principally in London, from which they could borrow dollars against which (because it was seen as a book-keeping transaction within each bank concerned) no reserves were required – until the Federal Reserve imposed special requirements in 1969.

This brings us to the factor mentioned earlier that tends to reduce the banks' power to frustrate the intended effects of monetary policy. For if, as just implied, central banks are in a position to give direct instructions to the banks concerning their reserve practices, then the logic of orthodox theory suggests that the central banks are in an impregnable position. On a more general view, this power to give direct instructions is seen as creating a system of 'variable reserve ratios'.

In the UK, the Special Deposits scheme, under which the clearing banks can be required to make deposits with the Bank of England that do not qualify for inclusion in liquid assets as officially defined, amounts to a 'variable liquid asset ratio' system – if there is a call to Special Deposits of 2 per cent of total assets, then the *effective* minimum liquid assets ratio is raised from 28 to 30 per cent. Again, however, we do not dwell on this aspect for reasons already specified. So far as concerns the cash ratio, the position is that the Bank of England's powers are in theory unlimited – since it can give directives to the banks under the 1946 Act – but in practice the 8 per cent ratio has been maintained for a quarter of a century, and certainly there is no formal scheme for its variation.

The Federal Reserve in the US, by contrast, does have such a formal scheme. By legislation of 1933, the Federal Reserve is empowered to vary reserve requirements against demand deposits, between the extremes of (in recent years) 10 and 22 per cent for commercial banks in the most important financial centres, and between 7 and 14 per cent for banks elsewhere; requirements against time deposits for all banks can be varied between 3 and 10 per cent. While the ratios are often not varied for quite long periods, in most recent years some change has been imposed.

So, in principle, the Federal Reserve could use this power to prevent the commercial banks from frustrating its intentions. If the banks reacted to a reserve squeeze by allowing their reserve ratios to fall, so that advances and deposits could be maintained, then all that is required is that the minimum reserve ratios should be raised close to the actual existing levels. Further, and again in principle, a squeeze on deposits could be imposed directly through raising the minimum requirements *above* the existing levels, forcing the banks to call in loans and so bring about cancellation of existing deposits.

The foregoing describes, we have said, the position 'in principle'. In practice, the Federal Reserve, in raising reserve requirements, has tended to confine itself to neutralizing existing holdings of excess reserves, just as the Bank of England has used its powers under the Special Deposit scheme to reduce the clearers' effective liquid asset ratio *towards* rather than *below* the 28 per cent minimum. (It will be observed that we have begun to move towards discussion of similarities between the two countries rather than contrasts between them, and so to arguing the case foreshadowed in the second paragraph of this appendix.)

If we ask why the two central banks should have observed what is to all appearances an unnecessary self-denying ordinance, then we approach what this book argues to be the heart of the central banker's problem. For if a central bank were to raise the commercial banks' minimum reserve ratio(s) below the existing levels, then – to the extent that the central bank was the *sole* source of reserves (see above) – the commercial banks would need to borrow from the central bank as 'lender of last resort' if the minima were to be observed and public confidence to be maintained. In other words, the central bank would be forced to fulfil its *support* function, and in so doing would be offsetting the effects of its actions in execution of its *control* duty. This is the heart of the dilemma that seems to be unavoidable for central bankers whatever the differences in their institutional environments.

The argument for this proposition is strengthened when we consider another similarity between the UK and US systems, one that is of fundamental importance and applies – so far as the author's knowledge extends – to all advanced financial systems. In both the UK and the US, certainly, there exists an active and efficient money market made by dealers who accept short-term loans from transactors who are in (more or less) temporary surplus, in order to finance (perhaps slightly longer-term) advances to transactors in temporary deficit. The function of such money markets is frequently described by authorities as being to 'mop up' pools of idle funds and put them to active use. This function has often been argued as being useful and indeed essential for effective central bank control of credit, for obvious reasons. Unless the central bank can be confident that restrictive action on the reserve base will be transmitted quickly to the supply of loans from the banking system (and other lenders, on which see Chapter 6), then it cannot be sure of affecting either the quantity of bank credit or its cost. And the existence of pools of idle funds that could be mobilized by the banking system to sustain its lending activities, or tapped directly by borrowers unable to obtain bank loans, would militate against conditions conducive to such confidence; there would again be a strong probability of what we have described as 'slippage' in the system.

So, the money market's activity in mopping up idle funds can be represented as being conducive to effective central bank control of the banking system. But here, the perceptive reader might have noted already, a strong counter-argument might be advanced. For we may recall the earlier discussion concerning the problems encountered by central bank control policies in sectors of the financial system that do not contain pools of idle balances. Within such sectors, central bank security sales, designed to contract the banks' reserve base, can only be absorbed if transactors sell other assets. And if the central bank were to raise reserve requirements instead of making open-market security sales, then the commercial banks would be pushed into selling securities – again to transactors who would need to finance the purchase by selling some of their existing holdings.

Either way, therefore, we would be up against the problem whose analysis we have begun in Chapter 2 and shall continue in Chapters 3 and 4; in every such case there is the necessity of analysing reactions in the markets from which funds have been withdrawn in order to finance purchases of assets being unloaded by the central or commercial banks. In every case, there is the possibility of spiralling interest rates unless idle balances *are* somehow mobilized or unless some transactors are induced to reduce their expenditures and their demands on the financial markets. And in every case known to the author, spiralling interest rates create strong problems for central banks and strong pressures to switch over to giving the support function priority over the control function.

The argument can, indeed, be extended beyond the financially advanced economies specified at the beginning of this appendix. So much was in fact implied in the reference three paragraphs back to the functions of highly developed money markets. As there stated, in the absence of such markets, the existence of pools of idle funds is liable to create considerable difficulty for central banks. But there is a further complication in that central banks in developing economies tend to be committed much more consciously and explicitly to the support function, by virtue of their acknowledged task of fostering the development of financial markets. The merit of pursuing this objective is usually seen as residing in the idea that economic development is assisted by the availability of markets through which funds can pass from savers who lack entrepreneurial ability to those who possess acumen in production and distribution of goods and services but lack financial resources. The argument for central bank assistance in this sphere is that wealth-holders will not develop willingness to hold risky (especially long-term) financial claims if the prices of such claims are observed to be volatile in the downwards direction. So, the central bank has an inducement to 'support the bond market', with implications for the potentiality of monetary stabilization policy that should by now be abundantly clear.

Even in some economies that are highly developed on the 'real' side, such as West Germany and France, the liquidity-preference of wealth-holders is so strong that they tend to hold high proportions of their wealth in the form of claims on banks and similar financial intermediaries, so that these institutions tend to bulk large in the supply of long as well as short-term finance to companies. Because this situation is seen as having undesirable aspects, in these countries, too, there are many indications from official pronouncements that the central banks are concerned to foster the development of markets in long-term financial assets through which funds can flow direct from ultimate providers to ultimate users. The main ways of giving practical expression to this concern are to refrain from policy actions that might precipitate large and rapid declines in asset prices, and to move in to slow down such declines as occur in the course of the autonomous workings of the financial system.

All this might suggest, and indeed in the past it was frequently argued, that the eventual maturing of financial markets was a development that would be highly favourable to central bank control action. Mature markets, it might be thought, would no longer demand special consideration in the framing and execution of monetary stabilization policy. Because of their absorptive capacity, central banks could operate in such markets to buy and to sell securities in order to affect the banks' reserve base, without provoking big price fluctuations and (partly in consequence) without fear of disrupting the markets' performance of their basic function of providing a reliable flow of finance to deficit (investment > saving) units.

It is the argument of this book that these optimistic hopes, however reasonable and persuasive they once seemed, have not been realized. And the basic reason is that liquidity-preference in financial markets is not stable, but subject, as Keynes emphasized, to sudden and rapid shifts because of changing expectations about the future in a world where uncertainty is pervasive, however difficult it might be to capture the effects of that uncertainty in a concise and tidy theoretical model. The difficulties of doing this are compounded by the fact that wealth-holders' expectations are formed (as Keynes again emphasized) not solely on a basis of careful weighing of indications from developments in the 'real' sector of the economy, but also, and perhaps primarily, on a basis of guessing the way in which expectations of other wealth-holders will move. So, the flow of finance for 'real' investment in the economy is, as Keynes said in a famous phrase, the 'by-product of a casino'. The support function of central banks can be seen as an attempt to reduce the gambling risks of participants in the casino's activities, in the hope of mitigating the effects of the wilder swings of optimism and pessimism that used to occur before central bank intervention, and in more recent decades have sometimes occurred in spite of it.

One final point to be emphasized here is that talk of instability of liquidity-preference is not *necessarily* to be identified with instability of preference for whatever assets might or might not be included in a definition of *money*. An exodus of funds from building societies into bank deposits can, as we have seen, create disruption in the mortgage market that might spread to longer-term markets if unchecked. But trouble can also start in longer-term markets – say, if an exodus of funds from bond markets into building society deposits makes it difficult or impossible for government or private companies to finance deficits by sale of appropriate types of financial claim. But this brings us into the area of discussion for Chapter 3.

CHAPTER 3

Monetary Policy: Long-Term Asset Markets

At the end of Chapter 2 proper we saw that, one way or another, it is probable that restrictive monetary policy will produce a situation in the long-term government securities (or 'gilt-edged') market that can be described as one of excess supply of securities at the initial (assumed equilibrium) interest rate. In the present chapter, then, we shall investigate the probability that the resultant upward pressure on *long*-term interest rates is more capable of restoring equilibrium with a reduced money stock than were the rising *short* rates of the analysis of the preceding chapter.

There are in principle two types of reason for supposing that this probability might be fairly high; the first relates to changes in the propensity to spend and the associated demand for active balances; the second relates to changes in the demand for active and/or idle balances in relation to a given level of spending. We may recall the earlier argument that one or more of these mechanisms must needs come into play if a new equilibrium with a reduced money stock is in fact to be achieved.

Taking the first type, we note that it is a widely accepted theorem that some types of investment expenditure are sensitive to changes in long-term interest rates; the theorem applies to spending on long-lived assets such as buildings, in respect of which interest costs tend to form a substantial proportion of the annual capital charges. However, it is also widely agreed that any effect on actual expenditures due to a rise in long rates is likely, owing to the long gestation period of this kind of capital project, to be delayed by many months. Accordingly, we cannot think of a reduced demand for active balances achieved by this path as a useful vehicle for policy-induced reduction of the actual money stock.

When we turn to the second type, we find that the analytical and practical considerations are a good deal more complex, and they will occupy us for the remainder of this chapter. The basic point here is that there are reasons for suggesting that the links with the pool of idle balances are stronger in the case of bands than in the case of public sector short-term liabilities. For the precautionary and speculative motives to liquidity are likely to be governed by costs of buying and selling, and by attitudes concerning possible or likely movements of yields on long rather than short-term assets. We might seem, then, to be back to the simple model of Fig. 1:8 and to the uncomplicated policy implications summarized on p. **00**.

However, if the real economic world were that simple, economists would be hard pressed to earn a living – and fortunately, for economists at any rate, the world is not that simple. We must recall our basic questions concerning the elasticity and stability of asset preference schedules and examine the gilt-edged market, especially the demand side, in more detail.

The opening stages of the argument are extremely similar to those of last chapter's analysis of the effect of excess supply and rising rates in the Treasury Bill market. To avoid the tedium of repetition, therefore, the reader may be left to develop for himself the following brief summary.

Baldly stated, then, the money/gilts margin portrayed in Fig. 1:8 is by no means the only margin across which asset-holders might switch in response to a rise in gilt-edged yields. Additionally, switches might occur in particular from the industrial debentures market and from the equity market. So to picture the process, we need to envisage rather elastic 'own-yield' demand schedules for each of these assets, placed against completely inelastic supply schedules because the total stock in existence must all be held by someone. And, by close analogy with our analysis of interaction between the Treasury Bill and local authority temporary money markets, we must suppose that a rise in yields on gilts that causes switches out of these other income-yielding assets will result in instability of the 'own-yield' demand schedules and thus in a tendency for yields to spiral upwards.

It follows that we need to visualize the situation in terms of less elastic 'all yields rising' asset-preference curves for gilts and other

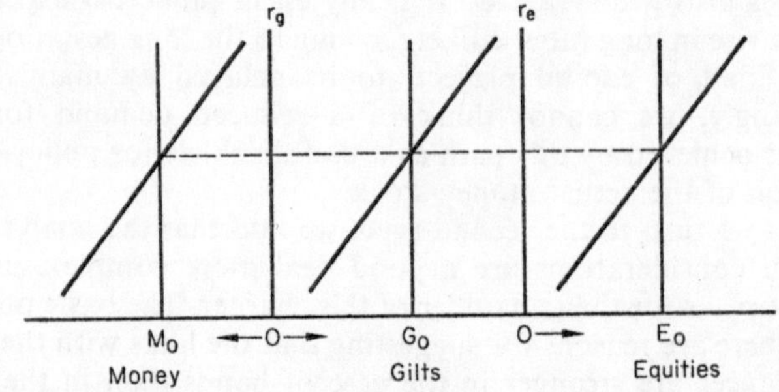

FIG. 3:1

long-term assets – of which we shall take equities as the most important example. So we have the situation shown in Fig. 3:1. The (dividend) yield on equities (r_e) might be above or below the yield on gilts (r_g), but is shown as equal to it for simplicity.

It can be seen, then – we are repeating, but the point cannot be overstressed – that the condition for achieving reduction in the money stock is that the 'all yields changing' preference schedule for gilts, and the associated money preference curve should:

(a) have enough *elasticity* for an adequate amount of switching from money balances into gilts (as well as other income-yielding assets) to be induced by a rise in yields that is tolerable to the central bank – given the existence of any constraints of the kind to which attention has been drawn earlier;
(b) be *stable* in the face of rising yields.

On (a) we shall say little at this stage. The issues are more empirical than analytical, and we shall argue later that such issues are extremely difficult of solution. On (b) there is more room for analytical and conceptual discussion of the sort to which this book is primarily directed.

Stability of demand for long-term assets

To begin with, it should perhaps be re-emphasized that, given the usual Keynesian assumption that the flow of savings and therefore the demand for a stock of wealth is insensitive to the rate of interest, the elasticity of the gilt (and equity) schedule(s) of Fig. 3:1 is *entirely* due to asset-holders' willingness to vary the proportions between money and other assets in their portfolios. This willingness is of course based, in Keynes's liquidity-preference argument, on holders' assessments of the relation between present yields and expected future yields. (This relation is the main influence on stability of preference schedules for long-term assets, and we shall concentrate on it here despite the fact that we have noticed other theoretical reasons that have been advanced for willingness to switch between money and interest-bearing assets.) Keynes himself argued that this dependence of asset-preference curves on expectations would tend to cause considerable instability, but this aspect of his argument has received relatively small emphasis in subsequent discussion. Because of its importance to the present problem, we must examine the matter more closely.

It is convenient to begin an analysis of the effect of expectations on the gilts-preference schedule by imagining first a situation in which expectations were irrelevant, say, because the market is absolutely certain that present yields will not change during its relevant time horizon so that no fear of capital loss or hope of capital gain on sale of gilts is in prospect. In that case, the considerations advanced in the previous paragraph suggest that it would be reasonable to think of the Keynesian argument leading to an absolutely inelastic demand schedule. (Remember that we have excluded substitution effects by virtue of our concentration on what is argued to be the realistic 'all yields changing' case.)

To introduce expectations into the picture, we now suppose that a long period of stability of yields is followed (for reasons our taxonomic argument need not specify) by a rise in yields (fall in prices). This rise may be supposed to effect market expectations in some way. We next ask what sort of effect there is likely to be, and whether it suggests that the preference schedule incorporating expectations will have a positive slope, as in Fig. 3:1, or a negative slope. For this purpose we may divide market operators, conceptually, into two groups.

The first group consists of transactors who have a firm notion of a 'norm' for long-term interest rates from which any departure would probably be temporary. We may call this group 'norm believers'. These transactors would tend to *purchase* additional bonds to add to their portfolios, in order to reap the capital gains that would accrue when yields fell back again. Such purchases might be financed in part by reducing money holdings, and such behaviour is of course highly desirable from the standpoint of a central bank seeking to control the money stock.

However, we must note the possible existence of a second group who lack any strong notion of a norm for long rates and whom we may call 'sceptics'. This group might well fear that the price fall will be repeated, and will have a strong inducement to *sell* gilts from their portfolios. In actuality their calculations would be greatly complicated by questions of tax liability and dealing costs (monetary and non-monetary) but we may illustrate the general point by means of a simple example that ignores such complications. Consider the situation of a holder of 2½ per cent Consols, the price of which has declined in the previous month from 51 to 50 (current yield 5 per cent). If he thinks the price fall likely to continue at the same rate, so that the price a month hence will be 49, he will in that one month suffer a capital loss equal to about 2½ months' income. He may of course be a long-term holder who does not have to worry about short-term book losses, but even so he can improve his position by a sale and than a repurchase after the price fall has ceased.

What happens to the market's desired stock of gilts as a result of the rise in yields thus depends on the relative strengths of the reactions of norm believers and of sceptics. If the former predominate, the desired stock will increase; if the latter, the desired stock will decrease. The (Keynesian) positively-sloped schedule was based on the idea that norm believers do predominate, and that they do so to an increasing extent the larger the movement of yields away from the notional norm.

In assessing the validity of this idea, we need of course to ask on what factors the notion of a norm is likely to be based. And the answer is that, though the market may from time to time be influenced to re-assessment by such extraneous factors as current government policies, prospects for the balance of payments and so on, the major factor will be past experience. The above assumption of a yield change following a long period of stability, therefore, might be regarded as having 'loaded' the argument in favour of the Keynesian solution.

This solution was in fact evolved against a background of very considerable long-period stability in long-term interest rates. Though Keynes in the 1930s was writing in an era disturbed by war and post-war upheavals, he (and, probably, the market) saw the long rate having returned to about 3 per cent, and looked back to a period between 1820 and 1914 during which the yield on Consols had fluctuated but little around a gentle downward trend running from around 3½ to around 2½ per cent. The grounds for regarding a rate around 3 per cent as at least a 'non-crisis' norm were therefore rather strong.

The last two decades, however, have seen an unprecedented upward trend that has carried long rates from around the old norm in 1950 to levels in excess of 9 per cent at the end of the 1960s. In these circumstances, it seems intuitively safe to say that the idea of a norm for long rates has virtually disappeared from market calculations. Particularly during the later part of this period, the rate has broken through one level after another that was regarded in prospect as a probable ceiling. The upward trend clearly must have some limit, but few would care to record their forecast of just where this limit will be found. There is nothing intrinsically impossible about long-term government stock yielding, say, 12 per cent or even more.

In these circumstances there is clearly a strong possibility of a rise in yields being accompanied by a decline, rather than by an increase in the market's desired stock of gilts, because of the effects on the calculations of the (?now ubiquitous) sceptics. It does not make a great deal of difference whether we think of such a development in terms (cf. Fig. 3:1) of a leftward shift of a positively-sloped schedule, or in terms of a schedule that in certain ranges and at certain times is negatively-sloped, though it will facilitate continuity of exposition if we adopt the former solution.

In terms of Fig. 3:1, however, with total (financial) wealth given, leftward shifts in the gilts-preference schedule might be accompanied either by leftward shifts (= greater liquidity preference) in the money-preference schedule, or by rightward shifts in the equity schedule. More probably, indeed, the main alternatives might be stated as either leftward shifts in both money and equity schedules, or rightward shifts in both schedules. That is to say, a situation in which there is a (net) market movement out of gilts might be one in which asset-holders in general are seeking greater liquidity, or one in which liquidity preference is declining. The former situation is likely to reflect doubts about the general economic outlook and fears of widespread declines in financial asset prices. The latter situation is likely to reflect an inflationary psychology causing asset-holders to seek protection against depreciation of the real value of their capital and income, and of course describes pretty well one of the basic reasons for the trend rise in long rates mentioned above.

We are now a long way from the simplicity of Fig. 1:8 and the simple policy implications sketched at the beginning of Chapter 2. But our conceptual discussion at least provides a framework within which to organize thought on the problems that face the central bank in practice, and it is to the history and prospects of the practical aspects of the problem that we now turn.

The essential nature of the central bank's practical problem is perhaps best thrown into clear relief by picking up a phrase from the last paragraph but one that perhaps reads rather strangely. What is the practical implication of the reference there to the possibility of 'a (net) market movement out of gilts'? How can the market achieve *net* sales of gilts?

If we think of *equity* holders selling, we usually assume that other market transactors will be buying the securities, albeit at reduced prices; the physical stock of securities in market hands is unchanged, although its total market value is reduced. (For clarity of thought, therefore, it is worth realizing that the absolutely inelastic supply schedules of Fig. 3:1 refer to physical quantities (Q), not to market values (quantity multiplied by price, $Q \times P$); thus, we have here a contrast with the supply schedules in short-term markets considered in Chapter 2, the contrast being explained by the fact that the long markets are not residual sources of finance satisfying borrowing needs that oscillate *from day to day*, nor is the need to refinance maturing debt a *constant* preoccupation of borrowers.) But in this case, of course, *net* market sales of equities would be impossible unless we chose to define the market non-comprehensively by, for example, excluding the banks; on any comprehensive definition, every sale would be balanced by a corresponding purchase.

The UK clearing banks do not of course hold equities other than by way of trade investment in, for example, hire purchase subsidiaries. But in the case of gilts we could make sense of the idea of net market sales by defining the market to exclude the banks and thinking of the banks making net purchases at falling prices. In the *increased* liquidity-preference alternative sketched three paragraphs above, this would also make conceptual sense because it would increase the money stock absolutely, as well as relatively to a declining market value of non-bank security holders' stocks of income-yielding assets.

When we turn to practicalities, however, the difficulty with this notion is that the banks – even if their cash and liquid assets ratios were above the minimum, making possible an expansion of higher-earning assets – are not immune from the calculations described in the foregoing classification of operators into norm believers and sceptics. On a falling market, the banks also might well be deterred by the prospect of book losses (even though they could – until 1970 – use their inner reserves to avoid disclosure) from buying gilts; unless, which is unlikely, they had stronger reasons than the market for being norm believers.

Official dealings in gilts

From all this, it follows that we can only think in realistic terms of the possibility of net market sales of gilts if the Bank of England itself is purchasing as agent for 'the authorities' (i.e. the Bank and the Treasury). The question, therefore, is why the authorities should consider making such purchases, bearing in mind that the context of our discussion is an attempt by the authorities to secure a reduction in the money stock by open-market security sales; purchases would of course undo the effects of the initial sales.

The basic answer to this question is that the authorities need to have regard to the market's willingness to hold gilts in the longer term. Only if the stock of gilts was known to be stable not only in the short period but also indefinitely, and if it consisted solely of irredeemable securities, could the authorities totally ignore this consideration, and contentedly leave the market to find its own equilibrium level whatever that might be. In reality, of course, the authorities know that they must be able to sell debt to cover any future budgetary deficits; and they know that, as existing securities mature, they must be able to refinance the debt by selling new securities (unless the budget is in adequate surplus) if they are to avoid being forced to borrow short from the banking system and so exert upward pressure on the money stock.

It follows that the authorities have an inducement to prevent such large declines in prices of existing issues as might be likely to damage the market's willingness to buy new issues as and when their sale in the future becomes necessary. The strength of this inducement depends on many factors of which perhaps the most important are:

(a) the size of the national debt in relation to the community's total wealth stock;
(b) the proportion of the national debt held by the domestic banking system;
(c) the volume of securities due to mature in the short and medium terms;
(d) the likelihood of future budgetary deficits;
(e) the strength of the link between current price declines and the market's future willingness to absorb debt.

Of these factors, (a)–(c) are quantifiable, and their tendency in the UK is to motivate the authorities towards preventing sharp price declines. On (a), the financing of two world wars and of that part of the investment of the nationalized industries for which internal finance was not available have left a national debt that bulks considerably larger in relation to total wealth than is the case in many other countries. On (b), a proportion of the order of a mere 10 per cent of the total debt is held by the domestic banks, so that any large-scale shift out of government debt that necessitated refinance by the banks could exert considerable upward pressure on bank deposits. On (c), maturities are frequently in excess of £1,000 million per year. Factors (d) and (e) are non-quantifiable. On (d), however, the tendency for public sector spending to rise faster than national income, combined with arguments that tax revenue as a proportion of national income is approaching or has approached the tolerable ceiling, might well be regarded as underlining the probability of future deficits in the longer term.

So much is probably common ground to most commentators. It is when we come to the really fundamental point (e) that there is room for real differences of diagnosis and of prescription. This matter has in fact been the subject of a dispute in which the authorities on the one hand, and many academic economists on the other, have tended to take different sides. Further, under the pressure of events, the authorities have in recent years made substantial shifts in their tactics, some of which at the time of writing (early 1970) are very recent. The position is thus extremely fluid, and some description of its evolution will be a useful prelude to a judgment that at this stage cannot be other than provisional.

What we may call the 'original' position of the authorities was spelled out in evidence to the Radcliffe Committee in the late 1950s and summarized in the Bank of England *Quarterly Bulletin* in June

1966. Essentially it rested on two propositions whose force may be understood readily in the light of our previous conceptual discussion. These propositions are:

(i) that investors in gilt-edged stocks tend to have rather short planning periods; e.g. in buying, say, a twenty-year stock, an insurance company's chief consideration will be the expected overall yield in terms of income plus change in capital value over a period of weeks and months rather than of years;

(ii) that investors tend, in the language used above, to be thoroughgoing sceptics rather than norm believers; i.e. any movement in yields, up or down, is thought likely to continue without limit, or at least without any close or ascertainable limit.

It followed that, in the authorities' view, the market was – on the convention we have already adopted – highly unstable; rising yields would shift the preference schedule towards the origin, and falling yields would shift it outwards from the origin. If it be asked why, in this case, the trend should ever change direction, resort was had to those extraneous factors affecting market confidence arguably not open to substantial influence or control by the monetary authorities, although probably susceptible to influence in some degree by fiscal policy.

In these circumstances, the policy followed by the authorities was designed to foster confidence by preventing large, quick declines in prices of gilts, i.e. on a falling market, the authorities exerted a brake by purchasing gilts from the market. Partly because large and quick increases in prices were also viewed with disfavour, but more strongly because of the constant pressure to sell (especially long-term) debt outside the banks, any tendency for prices to rise was also 'dampened', by official sales of gilts. That is to say, the policy was to 'lean into the wind' – whatever the latter's direction.

The implications for monetary control were clearly far-reaching. In a situation where restrictive policy was accompanied by excess supply of long-term public sector liabilities, the consequent downward pressure on prices was met by official purchases having the result of offsetting any effects from restrictive policies in the short-term markets. The outcome, then, was that quantitative monetary control was rendered largely impotent. And although rising interest rates should in theory tend to depress spending, if the view were taken – as it was by many, the Radcliffe Committee included – that spending decisions were but weakly responsive to rate increases, the conclusion was that monetary policy working through market methods (as opposed to direct controls) was a very feeble weapon of policy.

Academic criticisms

Because this general conclusion was widely shared by academic and other outside commentators, for several years debate was not joined on the rather technical question of the stability of demand conditions in the gilt-edged market. Many academics, however, never accepted the authorities' view on the technical question, their general scepticism about monetary policy being based rather on the ideas of interest-inelasticity of expenditure decisions and of borrowers' ability to switch away from particular channels (e.g. the banks) where lending was inhibited by direct controls. But when the general conclusion came to be questioned (see Chapter 7), attention became focussed on the technical issue.

The essence of the case made by academics unsympathetic to the official viewpoint can be summed up by saying that the situation could have been transformed either by more or by less official intervention in the market. The former view was perhaps more common in the earlier stage, and was argued in the Radcliffe report (cf. para. 576); the latter view has come into prominence more recently. We shall see that the two approaches have in common that they would result in considerably wider swings in rates than has policy based on the authorities' 'original' position.

The argument for *more*, or perhaps it would be better to say more active, intervention and management of the market in gilts can be summarized with the help of Fig. 3:2. Section (a) of this figure visualizes the difficulty as arising from the market's tendency, under the domination of sceptics, to project current rate trends and so not to be lured into purchasing as yields increase because of fears of capital losses. The problem facing the authorities would be – see section (b) – to inhibit such projection by changing market expectations about the future course of yields and prices. This would require that the authorities set a ceiling to the rate (= a floor to bond prices) at an appropriate level, which in turn would necessitate making their intentions obvious to the market by producing a quick rise in the rate followed by stability – that is, you would get the step movement of section (c). The effect, then, would be to transform the smooth 'natural' schedules into step schedules – section (d) – with the authorities operating what is essentially an adjustable peg system, similar in principle to that obtaining in the foreign exchange market.

It will probably already be obvious to the reader what is the important condition that would need to be satisfied for such a policy to be successful in stabilizing the bond-preference schedule and thus facilitating (restrictive) monetary control. When inserting the peg

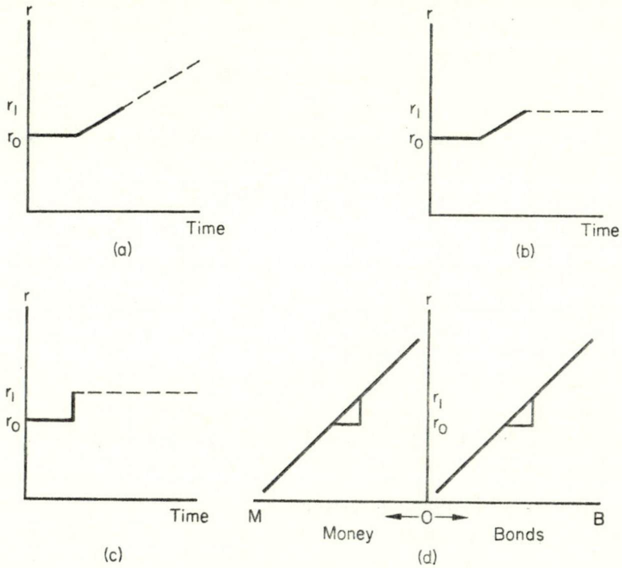

FIG. 3:2

at a new level such as r_1, the central bank would need to be confident of its ability to convince the market that this was a level that could, and would, be maintained for some time. Probing for the right rate by 'successive approximation' would be inadequate, for too frequent movement of the peg would destroy the whole basis of the policy. 'Too small' an adjustment would leave the market waiting for the remainder and moving out of, instead of into, gilts; analogies with exchange markets and the arguments for any adjustments of basically 'fixed' rates to be substantial readily suggest themselves.

In the exchange market case, some argue for complete absence of official intervention and so the analogy can be pressed further in describing the argument for facilitating monetary control by *less* intervention in the gilt-edged market. This argument is quite simply that there *must* be some level of yields at which the market will hold the total stock of gilts. If, in terms of Fig. 3:2, a rise in yields from r_0 to r_1 would be inadequate, then there must be a yield level above r_1 that *would* be adequate. Therefore, the best thing for the authorities to do is to leave the market alone to establish the appropriate yield level.

Changes in official tactics

For the types of reason we have described earlier, completely rigorous adherence to this policy is probably impracticable. The recent adjustments to official tactics in the gilt-edged market have represented tentative shifts in the policy's general direction. The Bank of England first revealed (*Quarterly Bulletin*, March 1969) that it was intervening less readily and automatically to steady movements in yields; and then (in September 1969) that it would no longer announce an official price at which it would be prepared to sell 'tap' stocks (i.e. stocks of particular securities which are held in the assets of the Issue Department of the Bank, ready for sale as and when market demand materializes) but would stand ready to receive bids made by the market.

These forms of words, of course, leave the precise extent of the actual change in the authorities' tactics in the market an open question. That the first change *is* significant but the second should not be exaggerated, is suggested by the following extracts from a paper prepared in the Bank in consultation with the Treasury, presented in October 1969 at a conference call 'Radcliffe – ten years after' (see *Quarterly Bulletin*, December 1969):

> 'In some cases official judgment has favoured moderating considerably any movements of interest rates; in other situations, however, where the market was tending to move in a manner considered to be an appropriate adjustment to current conditions, official intervention has been on a very limited scale, allowing market forces to be much more fully reflected in prices. In the last years of the period, as greater weight has been placed on monetary policy, there has been a greater flexibility in policy on interest rates and a greater willingness to allow upward pressures on rates in the market to take effect . . . but even with yields at the historically high levels of the recent past, it was not at all clear that official sales of stock would have been increased in the short term by lowering prices still further, and the long-term effects of such tactics would certainly have been harmful. In short, official operations in gilt-edged continue to be constrained both by the underlying market situation and by long-term concern for the maintenance of a broad market.'

So, the authorities appear to have made some limited shift in their policy stance – too limited, certainly, to satisfy the more extreme among their academic critics. Among the latter, it is possible to distinguish two (partly overlapping) groups.

First, there are the Quantity Theorists who argue that the authorities' intervention policy, far from strengthening the market's longer-term absorptive capacity, actually weakens it. The argument here is that gilt-edged purchases by the authorities result in increased money stock now; because of the strong (even if lagged) link between money stock and spending, the effect is to initiate or reinforce inflationary pressures; because inflation weakens the demand for fixed interest securities, future demand for gilts is depressed rather than increased. This chain of argument clearly depends on the validity of the idea of a strong link between money stock and expenditures. As we shall argue (Chapters 6–7) the case against this idea, we do not dwell on this branch of academic criticism.

Second, however, some econometricians have looked at the statistical evidence and have claimed to be able to discern patterns which suggest the existence of a functional relationship between demand for gilts and the yield on gilts that would be stable but for the effects of the authorities' own actions. On occasion, reference is made to policy actions outside the sphere of gilt-edged rate policy itself. For example, it has been argued (W. E. Norton, *Economic Journal*, September 1969):

(a) that calls to Special Deposits tend to be financed by bank sales of gilts – causing downward pressure on prices; but the authorities' policy of 'smoothing' movements results in gradual price declines, and this provides private sector holders of gilts with an incentive to sell now to avoid larger capital losses later;

(b) that 'requests' to the banks to restrict advances cause sales of public sector debt as an alternative means of financing expenditure, so that rising interest rates during a credit squeeze are accompanied by, but do not necessarily cause, reduced demand for gilts and similar assets.

So it is argued that if the authorities were to abandon 'direct controls' on credit of these types, and rely more strongly on market forces to sell debt and squeeze the money stock, they would perhaps be surprised at their own success.

It will be evident that such arguments must depend heavily on interpretation of observed 'facts' rather than on the 'facts' themselves. and indeed this is unavoidable because on investigation the attractive concept of a 'fact' in economics almost always turns out to be highly ambiguous. Clearly, such arguments concerning the effects of a fundamental shift in policy techniques are necessarily speculative. It is easier for outside commentators to advance the arguments than for policy-makers to decide to put them to the test; it is not the commentators who suffer if speculation turns out to be ill-founded. Policy-makers can hardly avoid moving slowly and experimenting very cautiously, tentatively assessing the results of a small experiment before moving further.

And here, of course, is encountered the unavoidable problem of the complexity of an economic universe in which many things change together, a complexity that makes confident interpretation difficult. Consider, for example, the 1968/9 experiment in permitting faster increases in interest rates. Certainly in the later part of the period, demand for gilt-edged has been more buoyant, thus providing evidence consistent with the theorists' contention in favour of stability of the gilts-preference schedule.

But on this evidence, two observations are in order. First, even the theoretical argument for stability is subject to the usual *ceteris paribus* clause. And in the relevant period, other potentially relevant factors have changed fundamentally, in a manner that might have been expected to push the gilts-preference schedule of Fig. 3:1 to the right. These factors can be characterized as what we have called 'extraneous factors affecting market confidence'. For example, the balance of trade was improving, arguably due to the 1967 devaluation of sterling and a long succeeding period of unprecedentedly tough fiscal and incomes policies.

Secondly, if extraneous factors have indeed affected market confidence in this (to the authorities) desirable direction, no one can guarantee that other factors will not soon operate in the opposite direction. For example, 'extraneous factors' such as a revival of strong hopes of growth on Britain joining the Common Market could precipitate a massive shift back into equities (and/or other inflation hedges such as real property) that no practicable rise in interest rates could stem.

It is too easily overlooked that the long downward drag on gilt prices has created a situation in which the demand for gilts for long-term investment purposes has shrivelled up. So, gilts are – as the authorities have argued – predominantly of interest to investors with (in respect of all or part of their portfolios) short-term time horizons. Such investors can be attracted into gilts in two types of situation:

(a) because rates are pegged by the authorities, or quick changes restrained, the securities are effectively rendered liquid assets, offering a good return on funds that are available for short period investment or might have to be sold to meet contingency needs;

(b) rates are confidently expected to fall, offering the prospect of near-certain capital gains that *will be realized once the fall in rates has occurred.*

High and stable rates foster type (a) demand. Volatile rates foster type (b) demand in *some* phases of the rates cycle. The authorities cannot encourage both types of demand with the same policies. Arguably, the critics are advocating tactics to foster type (b) demand without seeing the implication that, when rates reach bottom, the market cannot be relied upon to absorb new securities to meet a budget deficit or to refinance maturities. There are thus reasonable arguments for the authorities' continued caution.

On the other hand, it could be argued that if, whether by good fortune or superb economic management, such adverse 'extraneous factors' could be avoided for a period of years, so that the long downward slide in gilt prices was seen to have been decisively reversed, market sentiment towards gilts might be transformed. The result could be to reinstate the dominance of norm believers over sceptics. In consequence, long-term investment demand for gilts might blossom again. It may be doubted, however, whether the preconditions specified at the beginning of this paragraph are likely to be realized.

Overall, there seems as yet to be no strong reason for seriously modifying our earlier provisional conclusion, which can now be extended to the long markets. The central bank cannot escape from the twin duties of support and control. In varying degrees at different times, the conjuncture of circumstances causes these duties to conflict. In long markets as in short, the support duty emerges as fundamental.

The implication of the support duty is that the central bank is inhibited from exerting the sort of severe cash squeeze on the economy and the banking system that old and neo-orthodox policies would call for in a situation of strong inflationary pressures. Accordingly, the notion that the authorities can produce a reduction of £x in bank deposits by selling £0·08x of securities and relying on the bank credit multiplier process to do the rest must be rejected. So if, the argument of this chapter is valid, must be the weaker notion that official sales of £x of securities can always be pressed in order to reduce bank deposits by the same amount.

If accepted, this conclusion has more far-reaching implications for the theory and practice of monetary policy than may at first appear. For it is implied that there is, at least in the UK context, no real escape from the situation in which the banking system is the residual holder of government debt, obtaining the total minus whatever the private sector can be induced to hold. It would follow

(a) that a major means of influencing the banking system's holdings of government debt will be to change the total stock in existence, by working through fiscal policy;
(b) that the private sector is by no means bereft of channels by which to influence the total money stock in existence, contrary to the orthodox argument presented in Chapter 1.

The former of these dicta is explored in Chapter 5, and the latter in Chapters 6 and 7. First, however, there is a big gap in the foregoing discussion of the mechanisms of monetary policy, a gap to which attention is turned in Chapter 4.

CHAPTER 4

External Financial Linkages

Chapters 2 and 3 have argued that the mechanics of a restrictive monetary policy aimed at reducing the stock of bank deposits can be thought of as consisting essentially in the creation by the monetary authorities of a situation of (at initial equilibrium interest rates) excess supply of (income-yielding) financial assets. Even if this situation is created initially in short-term markets, in the traditional fashion, we saw that it was likely to have repercussions in long-term markets tending to reproduce the excess supply position there. Equilibrium can in principle be restored with a reduced money stock if the rise in interest rates associated with excess supply induces: (i) a *reduced supply* of securities by the private sector as spending is reduced and debt repaid, so that the need for active money balances is decreased; and (ii) an *increased demand* for income-yielding assets and a decreased demand for money as idle balances are activated or active balances economized. We have examined the various impediments to the achievement of this solution, summarized at the end of Chapter 3.

However, there is one other realistic repercussion of excess supply and rising interest rates that needs to be examined before this section of our argument is complete. So far, following convention in theoretical discussion of this particular problem, we have restricted the analysis to a closed economy with no external economic relationships. For almost any economy this would be an important omission; for an economy as 'open' in respect both of trade and of capital movements as is the United Kingdom, it represents *a priori* a large gap likely to produce erroneous conclusions. For, in such an economy, excess financial asset supply and rising interest rates must clearly be expected to attract fund inflows from abroad. It follows that we must find some way of integrating such inflows into our evolving conceptual picture. This will be the main objective of the present chapter.

At the risk, however, of causing readers to lose the thread of the main argument, we shall set this integration attempt into the context of a brief general examination of the domestic financial effects of external fund flows. For these effects clearly pose many problems for the 'theory and practice of monetary management' that is our general concern in this book; and they are frequently the subject of misconception in financial debate. Accordingly, we shall start the exposition of this chapter with general discussion of external financial flows, initially taking inflows as our example but all the arguments are reversible; and we shall work towards an answer to the specific question of the effects of an inflow of portfolio capital induced by rising domestic interest rates generated by restrictive monetary policy.

The effects of fund inflows: general analysis

The general argument is best conducted by abstracting at first from the highly important question of the causes of the inflow, and by taking as a point of departure the traditional theory that the domestic repercussions of an inflow will be substantial; or rather, that they will be substantial in a properly functioning system – the implications of this caveat are explained in the next section. Throughout this chapter we shall refer frequently to an inflow of 'gold', but this is to be understood as a shorthand term covering both gold and foreign exchange.

The traditional theory supposed that the 'natural' effect of a gold inflow was to produce an expansion of the domestic money supply, an expansion that could in certain circumstances be large in relation to the inflow that caused it. If we begin by visualizing a situation in which the money supply consisted entirely of gold coin, the basic point does not need to be laboured. The outcome is still quite simple in a situation where money supply is dominated by bank deposits and the commercial banks hold reserves with a central bank; but for purposes of using contrast to clarify the operation of the present UK system it is desirable for the possibilities to be spelled out somewhat.

TABLE IV. *Effects of changes in gold holdings*

	1	*2*		*1*	*2*
Clearing banks					
Deposits	10,000	10,050	Cash	800	850
			Other	9,200	9,200
	10,000	10,050		10,000	10,050
Central bank					
Public deposits	200	200	Securities	400	400
Bankers' deposits	800	850	Gold	600	650
	1,000	1,050		1,000	1,050

The main points that need to be appreciated are introduced by envisaging that the central bank holds the economy's gold reserve (gold is neither in circulation nor held in *commercial* bank reserves), so that a gain of gold implies – if the central bank is passive – an increase in the commercial banks' deposits with the central bank, these deposits of course forming part of their cash reserves.

We illustrate this in Table IV, using a very simple five-finger exercise, in which stage 1 represents an initial equilibrium position, and stage 2 shows the effects of foreigners selling 50 of gold to the central bank in exchange for (sterling) claims that are deposited with the (clearing) banks.

A little thought will make clear that partial equilibrium analysis of the orthodox bank credit multiplier type suggests a range of possible repercussions of which we may select three important cases:

(i) The central bank could do nothing, leaving the commercial banks to initiate a credit expansion in order to restore this cash ratio to the 8 per cent level. This expansion would have a theoretical maximum effect on bank deposits of 625 ($= 50 \times 100/8$).

(ii) The central bank could remove these *secondary* effects on the domestic money supply by selling 46 of securities from its portfolio, leaving the banks with the 804 of reserves required to support 10,050 of deposits.

(iii) The central bank could offset the effect on domestic money supply completely by an open-market sale of 50 of securities, restoring bank cash and therefore bank deposits to their original level.

Possibility (iii), which *in this partial equilibrium framework* represents 'complete insulation' against the effects of the inflow on the money stock, was of course contrary to the so-called 'rules of the game' of the gold standard as they were rationalized and simplified in academic discussion. In pursuing the traditional theory, therefore, we neglect it (though we shall need to return to it later). Of the other possibilities, (i) is the strictly logical outcome of conventional theory if the central bank is passive, but our general doubts concerning bank credit multiplier theory may allow us to envisage the central bank having an inducement to undertake support operations tending to produce solution (ii).

So we take an increase in M equal to the size of the gold inflow as the typical outcome of realistic partial equilibrium theory in the bank/central bank case just as in the pure gold coin case; for purely mnemonic purposes, we shall call this the 'natural effect'. From this point the classical price-specie flow balance of payments adjustment mechanism associated originally with David Hume relied on a Quantity Theory analysis to produce the causal chain: domestic expenditure and prices rise – exports fall/imports increase – adverse trade balance causes gold outflow tending to restore initial equilibrium. The Keynesian chain would have an additional link at the very beginning of this sequence, because domestic interest rates would fall as a result of the increased money supply. In both models, however, the whole sequence depends on the as yet unexamined assumption that the *demand* for money balances is static aside from the effects on it of the causal sequence itself (e.g. an increased demand for active balances) as demand for goods expands. We must, however, in our quest for greater realism in analysis, raise first the question of possible effects on the demand for money that are associated directly with the inflow. And to facilitate continuity we shall look at this question in the Keynesian framework.

From, as always, an assumed initial equilibrium position, we ask, then, why the demand for money might change as the direct result of some disturbance that also gives rise to a gold inflow. And the answer requires us to distinguish between two categories of disturbance:

(a) those having an effect on the levels of domestic output and income; and
(b) those having no such effect.

As simple examples of (a) we can instance a reduced propensity to import giving rise to a balance of trade surplus or an inflow of long-term capital for 'real' investment projects that would not otherwise have been undertaken; (b) can be thought of in terms of an inflow of

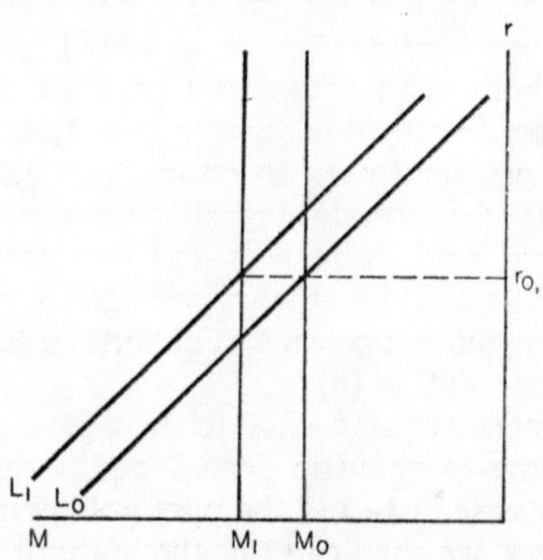

FIG. 4:1

'portfolio' capital due to foreigners having become more optimistic concerning prospects for the domestic economy.

The point of the distinction, of course, is that disturbances of type (a) will tend, via their effects on domestic income, to change the demand for active money balances. In the income expansion/gold inflow case, therefore, we shall have an increase in the demand for money as well as an increase in supply. There is no necessary reason, of course, why the two increases should precisely balance one another But in circumstances not wildly unrealistic, they could do so. Suppose, for example, that an improvement in the trade balance, representing an injection into the domestic income stream, were subject to an income multiplier of 2, and that the (stock) demand for active balances equalled half of the (annual) income flow; then the demand for active balances would equal the improvement in the trade balance – which, on our assumptions set out above, might well be a good measure also of the expansion in the money stock. So we would have (Fig. 4:1) a situation with no tendency for interest rates to change and no tendency for the balance of payments adjustment mechanism to be brought into play by strictly monetary forces – though as expanding demand forced up domestic prices the later stages of the classical/Keynesian sequences could operate.

Disturbances of type (b), by contrast, do not affect the demand for money directly; and so can be envisaged as in principle tending to be associated (in the case of an inflow) with a decline in the interest rates (Fig. 4:2) and with monetary impulses to balance of payments adjustment.

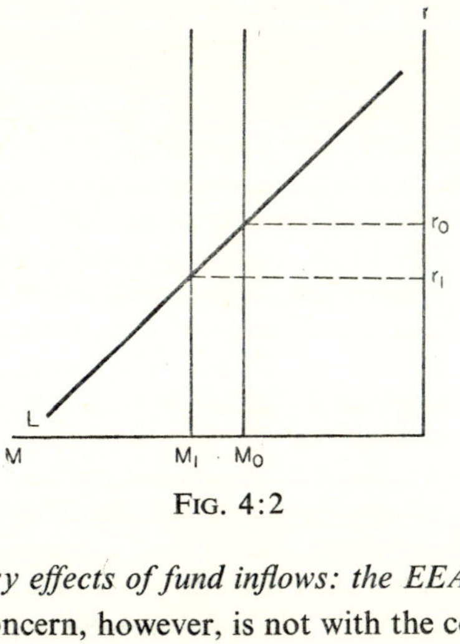

FIG. 4:2

Domestic monetary effects of fund inflows: the EEA System

Our primary concern, however, is not with the complexities of the external adjustment process but specifically with the domestic monetary effects of fund inflows (and outflows). And because, in our evolving picture, the domestic monetary situation is deeply affected by the preferences of holders of domestic financial assets, we are more directly concerned with type (b) disturbances. Such disturbances are particularly important for monetary management because their tendency, as Fig. 4:2 suggests, is to work counter to the objectives of domestic financial policy: *a restrictive policy aimed at reducing M and raising r may tend to attract a portfolio inflow having opposite tendencies.* Realization of these principles lies behind frequent assertions that the increasing integration of financial markets associated with such developments as the rise of the Euro-currency system has greatly increased the difficulties facing central banks attempting to tailor monetary policy to the needs of their domestic economies.

However, before we can evaluate properly the relevance of such assertions to the United Kingdom we need to move the argument into a more realistic framework. In particular, we need to take cognizance of an important respect in which the UK's institutional arrangements depart from those assumed in orthodox analysis of a 'properly functioning system'. Since the abandonment of the gold standard in 1931, the UK's external reserves have been held, not by the central bank, but by the government – though official foreign exchange transactions are conducted by the Bank of England as the operating arm of the monetary authorities. For book-keeping purposes these transactions are brought together in the so-called Exchange Equalization Account (the EEA), whose capital liabilities to the Treasury are balanced by assets in the form of gold, foreign exchange and Treasury Bills.

The mechanics of the operation of the EEA are in essence quite simple. They need, however, to be followed through rather carefully if their total impact is to be visualized clearly, and Table V contains a five-finger exercise to facilitate understanding. Because of the authorities' commitment to maintaining the foreign exchange value of sterling within narrow limits, an inflow tends to be absorbed by the EEA. The EEA buys gold and exchange for sterling deposits that are acquired by the sale of Treasury Bills from its portfolio. It is important to appreciate that this last sentence conflates two separate effects on bank cash that are mutually offsetting. The seller of gold to the EEA acquires a claim on the Exchequer that he can be assumed initially to deposit with a clearing bank, resulting in a transfer from public to bankers' deposits at the Bank of England and so an increase in the banking system's cash reserves (see Stage 2 of Table V). This increase, however, will be completely offset by the effects of the

EEA's concurrent sale of Treasury Bills; whether these Bills are purchased by the banks themselves or by other holders paying by cheque drawn on a bank account, payment for the Bills results in the Exchequer acquiring a claim on the banks' deposits at the Bank of England (Stage 3a/3b).

TABLE V. *Exchange Equalization Account operations* (£*m*)

	1	*2*	*3a*		*3b*		*1*	*2*	*3a*		*3b*
Clearing banks											
Deposits	10,000	10,000	10,050		10,000	Cash	800	850	800	(→805)	800
						Liquid assets	2,200	2,200	2,250	(→2,245)	2,200
						Other	7,000	7,000	7,000		7,000
	10,000	10,000	10,050		10,000		10,000	10,050	10,050		10,000
Bank of England											
Public deposits	200	150	200		200	Securities	1,000	1,000	1,000	(→1,005)	1,000
Bankers' deposits	800	850	800	(→805)	800						
	1,000	1,000	1,000	(→1,005)	1,000		1,000	1,000	1,000	(→1,005)	1,000

Under the EEA system, therefore, the effects of an inflow on the banking system's *cash reserves* automatically approximate to those in which a central bank holding the nation's external reserves offset gold acquisitions by security sales (case (iii), p. 100 above). However, our present more realistic argument cannot jump on to the case (iii) conclusion of abstract banking theory that the *stock of bank deposits* will also be unaffected. For we must take up the issue hinted at in the last sentence of the previous paragraph. The net effect of the EEA's operations in response to an inflow is to increase the stock of Treasury Bills to be held outside the public sector. The outcome for bank deposits depends crucially on whether these Bills end up in bank or non-bank portfolios. In the former case (3a) the banks acquire liquid assets to back and thus 'validate' the higher level of deposits shown in Stage 2, and make the small consequential adjustment to restore their cash ratio by selling back some of these assets to the Bank of England, as indicated by the figures in brackets. In the latter case (3b), deposits fall back to the initial Stage 1 level as purchasers of Treasury Bills draw on their clearing bank accounts to make payment.

Thus, 3a corresponds to what we called earlier the 'natural effect' case and 3b to the 'insulation' case. If we now ask which is the more probable outcome, we need to remind ourselves that, in the UK, the banking system is the residual holder of Treasury Bills. We may therefore conclude that 3a is probable (and is thus 'natural' in another sense) in situations where there is no special reason to expect a gold inflow to be accompanied by expansion of non-bank demand for Bills (or other varieties of government debt – see below). For examples of such situations, we may return to Fig. 4:1 and the accompanying exposition. It is true that if we have a trade surplus causing a multiplier expansion of domestic incomes, then savings are being made which will probably be seeking a home in financial asset-holdings, but we saw that the primary need in such circumstances is likely to be for a larger stock of active money balances. Fig. 4:1 and Stage 3a may thus be regarded as good approximations to the most probable outcome.

When we turn to the case, more important for our purposes, of an inflow of portfolio capital, the situation is different. For there is little reason to expect that overseas investors will wish to hold their new sterling funds in the form of clearing bank deposits, other than very temporarily. On the assumption that the inflow has been stimulated by a rise in United Kingdom interest rates, the funds are likely to seek investment in some other form of short-term income-yielding asset, and quite probably in claims on the public sector.

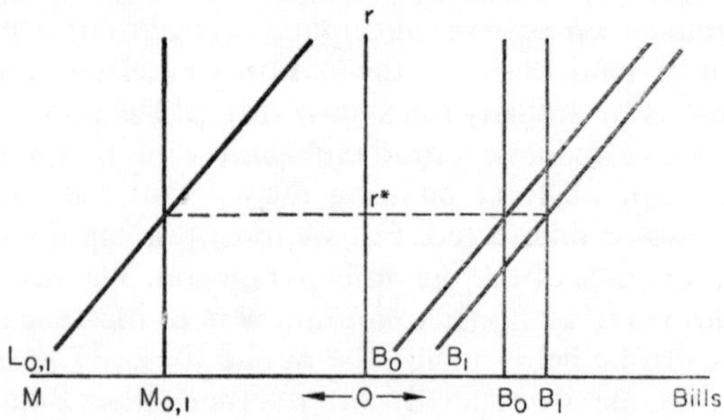

FIG. 4:3

If we take first the case of an inflow into Treasury Bills, we come to the important conclusion that Fig. 4:2 does not represent adequately the impact of the inflow. For what we have is a situation in which – as we have just seen – the supply of Treasury Bills has been increased by the operation of the EEA mechanism, and as a result of the inflow, demand for such Bills has increased by like amount. It follows that we can expect the 3b (insulation) outcome for the money stock and no net disturbance in the Treasury Bill market, as shown in Fig. 4:3.

On the face of it, this might seem to be a conclusion of some interest as a curiosity but of rather narrow practical application, given that portolio capital flowing into the UK has many possible destinations other than Treasury Bills. It is therefore of considerable importance to grasp the next proposition: that there are grounds for expecting the final outcome to approximate to that depicted in Stage 3b of Table V and Fig. 4:3 in a wide range of portfolio inflow cases. We may take, as key examples of such cases, inflows into local authority temporary money, long-term Exchequer debt and equities.

If short-term funds flow to local authorities, there are two channels by which effects might be transmitted to the Treasury Bill market to relieve there the situation of excess supply created by the EEA mechanism. On the one hand, if local authorities do not increase their borrowings in the temporary money market, the tendency for yields on local authority securities to decline might induce switching into Treasury Bills in the manner illustrated in Fig. 2:7. On the other hand if local authorities do borrow more temporary money, they might as a result borrow less from the Treasury via the Public Works Loan board – so causing the Exchequer's borrowing needs and the Treasury Bill issue to decline again.

If foreign funds enter the gilt-edged market in an inflationary period, when the authorities are trying to reduce domestic liquidity and bank deposits by debt funding, there will be a strong tendency for the new demand to be met by official sales. Rather than gilt-edged yields being forced down, therefore, the main impact will again tend to be a reduced Treasury Bill issue as the proceeds of the official sales are used to redeem short-term debt.

When foreigners purchase equities the seller will usually of course be in the private rather than the public sector. But the seller must do something with the proceeds of his sale. Should he use them to purchase some form of public sector debt, then one or other of the sequences above will tend to proceed in the same manner as if foreigners had bought public sector debt directly. If he makes a new purchase of equities, then some other transactor further down the line will quite probably be deflected into public sector debt.

One way and another, then, the chances seem quite high that the final outcome will approximate to that illustrated in Stage 3b (insulation) and Fig. 4:3. Of course, the direct flow or the deflection into public sector debt cannot be guaranteed to occur (and the complex chain of transactions could not possibly be traced in practice) so that some disturbance to the level and structure of domestic asset yields is possible. And even if the flow or deflection does occur, there are likely to be temporary disturbances to the yield structure whose effects are difficult to gauge. But we have arrived at the general, and important, conclusion that – contrary to the indications of abstract theory illustrated in Fig. 4:2 – portfolio inflows in the UK setting at least do *not* tend to exert strong effects on domestic liquidity and interest rates; and the reason is that the increased demand for financial assets tends to encounter a matching increase in supply. So we have yet another example of the way in which abstract theory represents a *starting-point* for practical economic analysis rather than supplying *conclusions* of direct practical relevance.

We conclude that the assertions concerning the technical difficulty or impossibility of conducting an independent monetary policy, to which reference was made earlier, are often based on misleading simplification of the true position. The assertions do have real force, but for reasons other than those frequently stated or implied; their force derives from two considerations that we have so far left aside. It is not the case that, if the UK authorities engineer a rise in domestic interest rates, the result is very likely to be an inflow that will expand liquidity and push rates down again. But it is true that, if a rise in rates here attracts funds from abroad, there will be repercussions in the overseas markets losing funds, that interest rates in these markets will tend to rise, and that we could get an international spiralling of rates of much the same kind as the domestic spiralling analysed in Chapters 2 and 3; therefore the UK authorities, far from finding it impossible to push UK rates up, might find themselves under some pressure, if securing an inflow were any part of their initial objective, to push rates higher than they originally intended. It is also true that, if the inflow were not desired, the gain to the gold reserves might weaken the authorities' will to pursue counter-inflationary policy at home – a point that can be seen to have more force in the reverse case of a portfolio outflow; the outflow probably does not force up domestic interest rates to any significant extent, but the loss of gold could impel the authorities to tighten domestic policy more than was desirable for purely domestic reasons.

Outflows and Exchequer finance

The outflow case has of course been all too common in the UK post-war experience, and it is desirable to notice an aspect of the operation of the EEA mechanism in such a situation that has attracted a good deal of critical comment, especially from this country's overseas official creditors. This aspect is that a UK deficit financed by sale of reserves or by borrowing results (as shown above) in the accrual of sterling to the authorities, which can be, and indeed normally is, used for the finance of public sector spending. The UK has on occasion been accused of 'pump-priming with her deficits', with the apparent implication that external deficits are seen as having inflationary domestic repercussions instead of the deflationary ones arising from the natural effect (a reduced money stock) in a properly functioning system.

On this criticism it seems proper to make three comments. First, although an outflow under the EEA system reduces the Exchequer's domestic borrowing requirement, an inflow increases that requirement; therefore, in so far as the critics are concerned to see that the overall stance of policy is deflationary in a time of secular creeping inflation they should at least concede that UK institutions offend only in periods of *continuing* deficit. Secondly, in so far as the criticism reflects any assumption that public sector spending in the UK has been higher than it would have been without the flow of 'easy' finance associated with prolonged deficit, the critics misconceive the operation of the UK fiscal mechanism; unlike some governments, the UK government's spending decisions are not constrained by limited ability (as opposed to limited willingness) to borrow at home. Thirdly, we have seen (Fig. 4:1 and supporting text) that even with a more 'orthodox' institutional mechanism operated on 'correct' principles, it by no means automatically follows that inflows and outflows generate strong monetary responses conducing to balance of payments adjustment; the orthodox analysis neglects the demand side of domestic financial markets.

It can thus be argued that the foundations of these criticisms are not strong. None the less, as in the case of official policy in the gilt-edged market, the views of critics among the UK's creditors have had some impact on the methods and objectives of policy. This impact can be detected in the concept of 'domestic credit expansion' (d.c.e.) first described publicly in 1969. This concept gives central place to the banks' lending to the public and private sectors and the associated change in the money stock. However, as the official proclamation of d.c.e. points out:

> 'a low level of borrowing from the banking system by the . . . government may be the result of a large amount of sterling accruing to the government in consequence of an outflow of foreign exchange' (*Economic Trends*, May 1969).

Accordingly, in interpreting developments in the monetary situation, there should be added to any increase in the money stock the figure for overseas lending to the public sector, including the sterling counterpart of any reduction in gold and foreign exchange reserves. The resulting figure shows

> total credit extended to the domestic economy by banks and overseas together.

Thus described, there seems to be no great harm in the use of the concept as an economic indicator, among other indicators, for interpreting past events. Its use as a target policy variable, and a key variable at that, is another matter for reasons discussed in the appendix to this chapter.

Conclusions

For the moment the need is to pick out, from this analysis of the domestic effects of financial flows across the exchanges, the thread that provides continuity with out main theme of the possibilities for restrictive internal monetary policy. And the point to note here is the negative conclusion of p. **000**. We may return to the situation sketched in the first paragraph of this chapter, with domestic interest rates tending to rise on account of a policy-induced excess supply of income-yielding assets. We ask ourselves about the implications of a possible inflow of portfolio capital stimulated by the rise in domestic rates – in more concrete institutional terms we can think for example of merchant banks borrowing Eurodollars and switching into sterling to offer funds in the local authority temporary money market.

The conclusion to be drawn from the argument of this chapter is that the implications are unimportant. The inflow will tend to benefit the reserves, and so could affect the stance of policy if the level of the reserves were one of the key indicators watched by the authorities. But it will not have much tendency to relieve the excess supply situation, and the tendency to an interest rate spiral, leaving the domestic banking system with fewer assets and fewer liabilities (deposits) in the manner predicted by orthodox bank credit multiplier theory. And the reason is simply that the increased demand for financial assets represented by the inflow will meet an increased supply.

From this it follows that the analysis of this chapter leads to no important modification of the conclusions set out at the end of Chapter 3. Contrary to much popular mythology, portfolio inflows do not, in the UK setting at least, make restrictive policy more difficult to operate. But neither do they, as we have now seen, make restrictive policy easier to operate. Although the student of monetary management needs to understand the reasoning behind these conclusions, we end by conceding that, for once, the limitations set by adopting the closed economy as a framework for analysis turn out not to be very serious.

APPENDIX TO CHAPTER 4

Domestic Credit Expansion

We have just pointed out that the figure for d.c.e. in a particular period can be regarded as showing

> total credit extended to the domestic economy by banks and overseas together.

Thus defined, it is not immediately clear whether what we have here is a CREDIT FLOW concept that picks out certain types of lending streams thought to be of special importance; or a MONEY STOCK concept that seeks to make some adjustment to the change in the money supply associated with bank lending, an adjustment designed to take account of the effects of external transactions.

Because of the complexity of the d.c.e. concept, understanding of it can be assisted by looking at the manner in which it is measured. We shall show that d.c.e. in a particular period can in fact be measured *either* as a total of certain credit flows *or* as a change in ('externally adjusted') money stock. And these two approaches to definition will be shown to underlie two corresponding interpretations of the concept's economic significance.

We turn first, then, to questions of measurement. We shall relate the exposition to the UK institutional setting so far as possible (remembering the special feature of UK arrangements, that reserves of gold and foreign exchange are held by the government rather than by the central bank). However, we shall make three simplifying assumptions:

(i) the relevant balance of payments concept is the 'basic balance', i.e. the balance on current plus long-term capital account;

(ii) there are no private short-term portfolio inflows or outflows, nor does the UK banking system borrow or lend abroad; the effect of this assumption is to ensure that the external surplus or deficit is accommodated solely by public sector transactions;

(iii) the public sector lends and borrows abroad only for purposes of settling such part of balance of payments surpluses or deficits as are not adjusted by changes in gold and foreign exchange reserves.

On these assumptions, we can use three identities to set out two approaches to measuring d.c.e., the approaches being those that underlie (A) the money stock and (B) the credit flow interpretations respectively.

(A) *Money stock*		(B) *Credit flows*	*Symbol*
(1) increase in bank deposits	≡	bank lending to (a) public and (b) private sectors	ΔM (for rows 1 and 2)
(2) increase in currency in circulation with the public	≡	finance provided to public sector by Bank of England Issue Department and Royal Mint	
(3) external balance	≡	change in reserves/public sector lending or borrowing overseas	ΔR

For both approach (A) and approach (B), d.c.e. in a certain period can be defined as (1) *plus* (2) *minus* (3). It might help to note specifically that an external *deficit* will be financed by a fall in the reserves and/or public sector overseas borrowing; (3) is negative, and we can think of d.c.e. as (1) *plus* (2) *plus* the balance of payments deficit. We shall first attempt to clarify the rationale of d.c.e. (or, at least one possible rationale) by explaining the theory that has been used to confer significance on approach (A).

It can be argued that, in an open economy, there is a case for making a distinction between two notions of the change in the money stock over a period of time. These two notions might be called the *ex ante* and the *ex post* change, in a manner somewhat analogous to the more familiar distinction between *ex ante* and *ex post* savings or investment. The nature and implications of the *ex ante/ex post* distinction in the money stock case can be explained by following through the following hypothetical causal sequence – assumed to begin from a situation of full internal and external equilibrium:

> (a) increase in money supply→(b) – by whichever of several possible 'linkage' or 'transmission' mechanisms – increased aggregate demand→(c) increased imports ∴ adverse trade balance→(d) loss of reserves/public sector borrowing overseas.

It is necessary to recall before proceeding that each of the alternatives at stage (d) results, in the UK system, in a flow of sterling finance to the government; this can be seen by reversal of the earlier argument for the inflow case. Given the total government (public sector) borrowing requirement, therefore, there is a likelihood that the Treasury Bill issue will decline, that the banks will get fewer Bills than would otherwise have been the case, and that the money stock will be lower than it would otherwise have been; cf. the reverse of Stage 3a in Table V. This linkage between external deficit and internal money stock would be more direct and certain in the context of the 'properly functioning system' where the exchange reserves are held by the banking system rather than by the government. The linkage is further examined below, but for the moment we take it as given.

We can now proceed with the exposition by using a very simple (and very hypothetical, let us remember) arithmetical example. Suppose that the original monetary expansion at stage (a) *ex ante* ΔM had been £500 million. Suppose that, as a result of the ensuing sequence of events, imports rose by £100 million, causing an adverse trade balance and a decline in the reserves of the same amount. The associated reduction in the money stock then leads to the conclusion that the change in that stock over the whole period *ex post* ΔM will be only £400 million. This is £100 million less than the monetary expansion that started off the whole process.

We can summarize the argument symbolically, using the formula given earlier. Let E represent d.c.e. in the relevant period. Then,

$$E = \Delta M - \Delta R \qquad (1)$$

In our arithmetical example, $E = 500$, $\Delta M = 400$, $\Delta R = -100$. Reference to the right-hand (B) side of the table might help to further clarify what is happening. We may assume that the banks initially lent 500 to private sector borrowers; the consequential developments eventually result in bank lending to the public sector falling by 100, so that the net increase in bank assets and liabilities is only 400. We might notice that when, as here supposed, the balance of payments is in deficit, $E > \Delta M$, so that a ceiling of £x million is more restrictive if applied to E than if applied to ΔM. Conversely, of course, if the balance of payments is in surplus $E < \Delta M$, and a given ceiling is less restrictive when applied to E; that is to say, money supply can rise by more than the d.c.e. ceiling.

So we see that, *given the hypothetical causal sequence here assumed,* it is E rather than ΔM that correctly registers the strength of the initial monetary stimulus. Thus it can be argued by those who lay stress on this causal sequence that E, the *ex ante* change in money, is the best measure of what is macroeconomically the important causal quantity. If M is the appropriate monetary concept and target policy for a closed economy, then E is the appropriate concept and target variable for an open economy.

As implied, the usefulness of this set of ideas depends on the validity of the macroeconomic theory underlying them. It is of course the Quantity Theorists who place most stress on the primary causal significance of the money stock, and on the strength and stability of the link between stages (a) and (b) in the sequence outlined above. In its purest form, the Quantity Theory leads to the assumption of stability in the income-velocity of circulation of money (Y/M, where Y represents national income). The simplest way of representing this stability in building up a formal model to replace the rough-and-ready theorizing we have used so far – a replacement that is necessary if the policy implications of approach (A) to the d.c.e. idea are to be appreciated fully – is to use as the analytical time period the income-turnover period of money balances. So we have:

$$\Delta Y = \Delta M \tag{2}$$

(If the income-turnover period is three months, then in one quarter – with constant velocity – Y will rise/fall by as much as M rises/falls.)

Academic Quantity Theorists have tended to content themselves with theorizing about the workings of a closed economy. Policy advisers using a Quantity Theory approach have had to be concerned, more realistically, with open economies. Economists at the International Monetary Fund have explored the implications of assuming strong and stable links between stages (b) and (c), and between stages (c) and (d), of our assumed sequence. The former link leads to the idea of the level of imports (I) depending solely on the level of national income; if this relationship does not change with the level of income, so that the average and marginal import propensities (m) are equal, we have

$$I = mY \tag{3}$$

The latter link gives us

$$\Delta R = X - I \tag{4}$$

Equations 1–4 above give us a complete working model of a simple economy. The reader can check for himself that the figures of our arithmetical example can be fitted to the model by assuming that X and I were initially zero, and that $m = 0{\cdot}25$; it might assist understanding to check what would happen if E were, say, halved to 250 per period.

The practical usefulness of this model depends on two factors, one rather obvious and the other more subtle.

First, the relationships summarized in equations 2 and 3 must indeed be highly stable. Empirical testing of the model for the UK has not proceeded very far, but with regard to income-velocity (equation 2) we may summarize post-war experience by saying that after rising substantially in the 1950s, velocity has in the mid and late 1960s fluctuated within a relatively narrow range. Even so, year-to-year movements have sometimes been significantly large. For example, using the 'wide' official UK definition of money supply that embraces time as well as demand deposits, and merchant as well as clearing banks, velocity fell by approximately 2½ per cent between 1967 and 1968, going some way towards offsetting any potential effects on aggregate demand from a money supply increase of 10 per cent. The imports-income relationship of equation 3 has also fluctuated a good deal; the proportion of total imports to GNP (market prices) was 14·4 in 1967 and 16·3 in 1968, a rise of about 14 per cent.

These matters are not further explored here, because it can be argued that the more subtle question underlying the model's usefulness is also much the more important one. It is also much more closely related to the subject matter and conclusions of this book. It will be clear on a moment's reflection that the model we have been examining makes the typical orthodox assumption that the creation of money by the banking system is under the authorities' control, i.e. that it is, from the standpoint of the private sector, an 'exogenous' variable. The departure from orthodoxy underlying the money stock interpretation of d.c.e. is relatively minor; it is assumed that the authorities can control E rather than M, because the extent to which a given E is reflected in a change in money stock on the one hand, and a change in external reserves on the other (equation 1), depends on the endogenous factors summarized in equations 2 and 3.

However, the notion of exogeneity of money implies that the private sector is the residual holder of government debt, i.e. that the central bank (by following an appropriate interest rate policy) can be sure of placing sufficient of the total stock of government debt with the private sector to ensure that the banking system is left with only that amount appropriate to the policy-makers' desired level of money stock. As stated at the end of Chapter 3, the argument of this book casts considerable doubt on the practical validity of this notion.

In the closed economy context of Chapters 2 and 3, this doubt arose from the pressures on the central bank to act in such a way as to modify tendencies for interest rates to fluctuate, in part because of the possibility of perverse reactions of private sector demand for public sector debt, a rise in interest rates being capable of affecting expectations adversely and causing the desired level of debt-holdings to decline rather than to increase. In our present open economy context, we can notice another factor that might strengthen this tendency to perverse changes in expectations. For if the central bank institutes a monetary squeeze or rising interest rates in a situation of inflation or balance of payments deficit, the weakness of the bond market is likely to be accentuated by the confidence effects of the weakness of the home currency in the foreign exchange market. In such circumstances, the inhibitions against an orthodox squeeze on the money supply being pressed very far are likely to be very strong.

What the authorities *can* do in such a situation is to institute a restrictive *fiscal* policy with a view, *inter alia*, to reducing the public sector borrowing requirement. This brings us, at length, to approach (B) to interpreting d.c.e., the credit flows approach. For a glance at the right-hand side of the earlier table shows that public sector borrowing is very prominent among the components of d.c.e. One way in which to attempt to remain within a given d.c.e. ceiling in the face of some tendency for private sector *demand* for government debt to decline, therefore, will be to use fiscal policy to reduce (either absolutely, or relative to what would otherwise have occurred) the *supply* of government debt in existence. It will be clear that such a policy might, *inter alia*, help to influence bond market expectations favourably, but judgment of the likely outcome must await detailed examination of the monetary implications of fiscal policy, to which we now turn in Chapter 5. We shall return to make our final observations on d.c.e. in the closing paragraphs of Chapter 7.

CHAPTER 5

The Monetary Implications of Fiscal Policy

After the extended discussion in Chapters 2–4 of the scope and limitations of an orthodox restrictive monetary policy in the situation in which the central bank takes the stance of government fiscal policy as given, we now turn to consider the alternative case in which fiscal decisions are taken with one eye specifically on their financial implications. There is, no doubt, a sense in which this alternative case is much more realistic, since it is hard to imagine financial and fiscal policies being formulated in complete isolation from one another – at least in the decades since treasuries and central banks perceived that there might be some gains from mutual discussion and co-operation. Certainly from the late 1960s onwards in the UK the financial implications of fiscal policy have been well to the forefront of policy-makers' minds. This does not mean, however, that in Chapters 2–4 we have been engaged in erecting and buffeting straw men. In earlier periods, monetary policy was regarded as so much subordinate to fiscal policy that it was a reasonable approximation to think of the central bank operating in a fiscal framework given, as it were, from outside. And academic discussion has centred almost exclusively on what we have labelled, as a shorthand term, the 'wealth given' case.

Not only for completeness, then, but also on account of its greater relevance in more recent times, we shall in the present chapter take up the 'wealth changing' case; the case in which fiscal policy is affecting the levels of income and saving flows, and therefore the wealth stock and the position of asset-preference schedules, in ways that clearly affect the environment of monetary policy. Within this context, we can distinguish two closely related problems for analysis. On the one hand, there is the general question of the financial repercussions of fiscal decisions and the possibility of feedbacks from financial markets to goods markets. On the other hand, there is the specific question of the authorities' ability to achieve particular financial targets (e.g. a given level of the money supply) by manipulating fiscal variables. As in Chapter 4, we shall provide a skeleton analysis of the general question by way of approach to an answer to the specific question. Happily, the whole topic can, for present purposes, be treated more briefly than was the 'pure' monetary policy ('wealth given') case.

Just because our new topic concerns situations in which the wealth stock is changing as a result of saving from income flows, we now need to recall the discussion of Chapter 1 concerning the interaction between financial stocks on the one hand, and financial and real flows on the other. The reader might at this stage wish to refresh his memory of the exposition building up to Fig. 1:6. We summarized there a conceptual sequence in which the major chain for our purposes led from a flow of bank loans, through the income-creating expenditures that they financed, to savings and to consequent shifts in the preference schedules for money and for income-yielding assets.

In that sequence, however, new injections of income-creating expenditures occurred solely by way of (firms') investment in plant, machinery, and so on; and households' saving constituted the only leakage from the circular flow of incomes. In considering an open economy in Chapter 4, we managed to avoid the explicit elaboration of this model, to show exports as an injection and imports as a leakage, which fuller treatment of external economic relationships would have required; this avoidance of complication was possible because we were able to conclude that external relationships did not affect the environment of monetary policy as radically as *a priori* considerations might lead us to suppose. But, as indeed has already emerged from our discussion in Chapters 2–4 of the implications for central bank policy of existing stocks of public sector debt, government finance does exert a fundamental influence on the financial environment.

Accordingly, it will assist our attempt to visualize clearly the complex interlinkages bearing on financial policy if we extend Fig. 1:6 by incorporating as an injection total government expenditure (G) and as a leakage total government tax revenue (T). But, to avoid unnecessary elaboration, we shall build into our picture only the net budget position, which in the case of a budget deficit gives us an additional injection represented by G-T (Fig. 5:1). The deficit may be financed, as the arrows indicate, by borrowing from banks; or by tapping savings, either current or past (idle balance mobilization). Borrowing from o.f.i.'s we shall in the interests of simplicity ignore for the time being – but we shall return to it in Chapter 6. In order to fully refresh the reader's memory of the discussion in Chapter 1, we reproduce the complete flow diagram, including the 'real' as well as the 'financial' circuit.

The reader should find no difficulty in using Fig. 5:1 to interpret

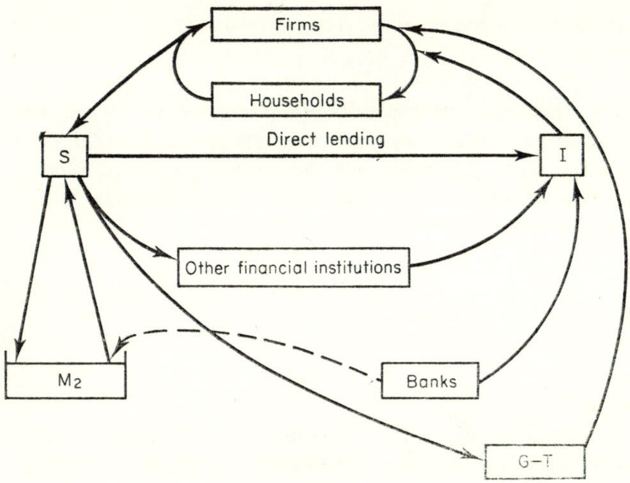

FIG. 5:1

the financial repercussions of a budget deficit in a manner similar to the earlier description of the effects of an excess of planned investment over planned saving. That description was, however, rather general, and, in view of the importance of the present topic for our overall theme, it will be desirable to spell out the argument a little more carefully. In so doing, however, we shall continue to operate with only that degree of complexity and rigour required to make plain the principles that affect the practice of monetary management.

The finance of a budget deficit: basic theory

Omitting some of the detail, the broad scheme underlying Fig. 5:1 can be embodied in a simple algebraic formulation. The formulation will be already familiar to many readers as an unlagged Keynesian model of a closed economy with government. G and I are determined exogenously. The government levies total taxes (T) at a rate (t) on pre-tax income (Y). Consumption spending (C) is a constant function (c) of disposable, post-tax, income (Y_d); s is the corresponding saving function. So we have:

$$G = G \qquad (1)$$

$$I = I \qquad (2)$$

$$T = tY \qquad (3)$$

$$C = cY_d = c(Y(1-t)) \qquad (4)$$

$$Y = \frac{I+G}{s(1-t)+t} \qquad (5)$$

The 'fundamental identity' of the model is

$$I+G \equiv S+T \qquad (6)$$

since total injections necessarily equal total leakages *ex post*.

For the benefit of the non-mathematical (among whom the author is numbered), we shall develop the exposition from here by using arithmetical examples. Suppose, then, that $s = 0{\cdot}25$, and $t = 0{\cdot}2$. Then the denominator of (5) reduces to

$$0{\cdot}25(0{\cdot}8)+0{\cdot}2 = 0{\cdot}4$$

The multiplier to be applied to $I+G$ in calculating Y is thus

$$\frac{1}{0{\cdot}4}=\frac{5}{2}$$

The financial effects of a budget deficit will stand out more clearly if we provide first, as contrasting background, a picture of the balanced budget case – in which, because all government spending can be financed from tax revenues, the government's fiscal operations cause no direct disturbance to the financial situation.

Suppose, then, we have an initial equilibrium situation, assumed to have endured for some time, in which $I = 50$, and $G = 50$. It follows that

$$\text{(a) } Y = 100\times\frac{5}{2} = 250$$

$$\text{(b) } G = 50$$
$$T = 50$$
$$\text{(c) } I = 50$$
$$S = 50$$

The financial implications noted in the previous paragraph are carried by (b). Although it is not central to our present concerns, we may note that (c) shows that household saving is adequate to finance firms' investment. If the channels used are direct finance of o.f.i.'s (Fig. 5:1) there are no monetary developments. If savers wish to use all or part of their savings for (net) accumulation of money balances, we have an increase in the demand for money which in the 'idle balance' case can be represented by a flow into the M_2 tank; disturbance is avoided only if the banks finance an equivalent portion of the investment expenditure by making new loans. If the banks were to make loans (create deposits) in excess of ΔM_2, there would be complications that our present simple unlagged model is inadequate to handle.

Our focus of interest for the moment, however, is the financial operations of the government. And we can begin to bite on the substance of the matter by supposing that the foregoing equilibrium position is now disturbed by an increase of G to, say, 54, with no change in the (marginal and average) tax rate (t).

In this case we would have $I = 50$ and $G = 54$, so that

$$\text{(a) } Y = 104 \times \frac{5}{2} = 260$$

$$\begin{aligned}
\text{(b) } G &= 54 \text{ (budget deficit} = 2) \\
T &= 52 \\
\text{(c) } I &= 50 \text{ (private sector financial} \\
S &= 52 \text{ surplus} = 2)
\end{aligned}$$

Let us note first that the budget deficit is smaller than the rise in G because tax revenues increase as incomes expand. The deficit is also precisely equal to the private sector financial surplus; this of course follows from the 'fundamental identity' of the model, set out in (6) above. If we then abstract entirely from the finance of firms' investment by supposing that, for example, firms' whole financing requirement is covered by direct borrowing from savers, we have the government needing to borrow 2, and savers with 'spare' savings of exactly equal amount.

The finance of a budget deficit: the range of practical possibilities

In principle, therefore, there is an adequate supply of savings that can be tapped to satisfy the government borrowing requirement. Appreciation of the principle probably lies behind the very widespread neglect, at least in the earlier years of the Keynesian era, of the financial implications of fiscal policy. However, we must notice that the existence of an adequate supply of savings is no guarantee against monetary disturbance, for reasons hinted at four paragraphs back.

The point is, of course, that savers may wish to use their 'spare' savings either to accumulate money balances (if for idle balances, flow to M_2 tank) or to purchase government bonds (or, of course, a mixture of the two, but for simplicity we shall stick to the extreme cases). We shall find it useful to illustrate three possibilities (Fig. 5:2), using a now familiar piece of apparatus.

Case (a) in Fig. 5:2 represents the situation in which savers wish to use their spare savings to accumulate additional liquidity, so that the money preference schedule (recall that, in the present framework, money and liquidity are synonymous, an assumption relaxed in Chapter 6) shifts outwards from the origin, from L_0 to L_1. If the government finances its deficit by borrowing from the banks, the money stock increases from M_0 to M_1 (= 2 in our arithmetical example). In the outcome, therefore, the demand for money and the supply of money at the equilibrium interest rate r^* have increased by equal amounts, so that interest rates remain undisturbed.

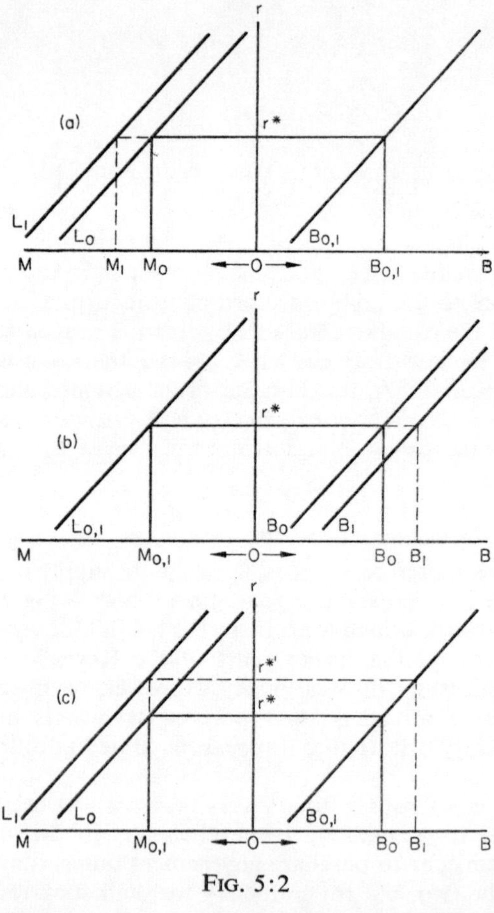

FIG. 5:2

If this argument based on the unrealistic timeless Keynesian multiplier model seems suspiciously slick, it is not difficult to express the essentials of the argument in more realistic form in a manner that carries conviction. We can think of a first stage in which the government finances its deficit by borrowing from the banks, so that banks' assets and liabilities (deposits) both increase. (If this borrowing is *not* effected by selling *long*-term bonds, of course, then the banks' cash and/or liquidity ratios would rise, implying the possibility of a multiple expansion of bank credit. But for the reasons expounded in Chapters 2 and 3, and further discussed in Chapters 6–7 below, we neglect this logical possibility as being of very limited empirical relevance.) As a result of the budget deficit, however, new incomes are generated from which savings accrue. The incomes will normally be received in the form of money, and if savers desire to add to their money balances, these balances become 'firmly held' and the initial increase in the money stock is 'validated'. If bank deposits are created as a by-product of loans to finance spending injections but savers' preferences do *not* allow the deposits to become 'firmly held', then again we have the interesting and important case referred to earlier, which we take up again later.

For the time being, we return to the simpler timeless multiplier framework to complete our examination of the range of possibilities for the financial effects of fiscal policy. Case (b) in Fig. 5:2 depicts a situation in which savers wish, at going interest rates, to devote their spare savings to the purchase of bonds, and the budget deficit is financed by the sale of new bonds. Once again, the outcome is zero disturbance to interest rates and zero 'feedback' from the financial to the goods markets. This absence of disturbance, it will be seen, is due to the fact that in both (a) and (b) the government in its borrowing operations (= issue of securities) exactly matches the preferences of savers in their purchase of securities.

By contrast, there will be financial disturbances, carrying the possibility of feedback effects on the goods markets, if the government – whether by choice or miscalculation – does not match the preferences of savers. Obviously, there are two extreme possibilities here, of which (c) in Fig. 5:2 illustrates one – the case in which savers wish, at the initial level of interest rates, to add to their money balances but the government (perhaps wishing to minimize the inflationary effects of its deficit by pursuing a restrictive monetary policy) finances its deficit by the issue of new bonds. In this case, interest rates must rise to induce asset-holders to accommodate their preferences to the mix of assets available. *Provided the asset-preference schedules are stable in the face of rising interest rates* (recall the argument of Chapters 2 and 3), the authorities can achieve their objective of preventing an increase in the money stock in spite of the budget deficit. If expenditure were sensitive to interest rates, of course, the feedback effects in the goods markets would themselves set up influences reflecting back again on financial markets, but these repercussions would probably be of relatively small magnitude and need not be followed through in argument at the present level of generality.

If the analysis of Chapters 2 and 3 is valid, the proviso in italics in the previous paragraph is a large one. That analysis would lead rather to the conclusion that, if a budget deficit is setting up influences tending to increase the demand for money balances, any attempt to offset this increase will tend to touch off an interest rate spiral. This spiral, given factors tending to inhibit the authorities from leaving interest rates to find their own level, is likely fairly quickly to bring the authorities in to support the markets in government debt, i.e. to purchase debt and so allow the money stock to increase. Therefore, (c) in Fig. 5:2 is not to be taken, in itself, as indicating that control of the money stock in the fiscal ('wealth changing') context is any easier than in the monetary ('wealth given') context.

Monetary effects of changes in fiscal policy

However, we have been discussing so far the financial repercussions of a *given* budget position. But we must notice that the discussion carries important implications concerning the potency for influencing the financial situation of a *change* in budget policy directed to that objective. This can be seen if we compare (a) and (c) of Fig. 5:2 with the balanced budget case discussed earlier, and imagine the authorities moving from a position of deficit to a position of balance with a view to (not, now, reducing but rather) avoiding growth of the money stock. The foregoing analysis clearly suggests that this manoeuvre is likely to be successful. For in eliminating the budget deficit, the authorities will be removing the influences (pictured in Fig. 5:2(a) and (c)) tending towards an increased demand for money. And if the demand for money does not increase, there is obviously much less difficulty in avoiding increase in the supply.

It will be clear that this argument applies, *mutatis mutandis*, to a budget deficit that is reduced rather than eliminated. It obviously applies *a fortiori* to a move into surplus that provides funds for the repayment of debt, because our analysis of the factors tending to cause instability of asset-preference schedules implies that the market's reactions are quite likely to reinforce a tendency for security prices to rise as well as a tendency in the reverse direction. Of course, if such factors as strong inflation fears were prompting sales of government debt, official purchases financed from a budget surplus might be inadequate to reverse an existing downward trend in prices, so that 'support' purchases and monetary expansion might still be required. But this expansion will be 'less than it would otherwise have been', so that fiscal stringency will still be tending to reduce the rate of growth of the money stock.

We have thus arrived at an important conclusion. If the authorities are willing to use fiscal policy in the interests of quantitative monetary control, they are likely to have considerable success. Concerning this success, however, two important observations should be made. First, as implied at the end of the previous paragraph, the authorities' ability to achieve a specific quantitative goal for the level, or rate of growth, of the money stock is doubtful, and much will depend on the background circumstances.

Secondly, and most importantly in the light of current controversies in monetary theory, it will be very difficult to assess the causal significance for aggregate demand in the economy of successful influence over the money stock achieved by manipulating fiscal variables. For, even if such a restrictive fiscal-cum-monetary policy appears to be successful in deflating aggregate demand, the problem of separating the *direct* deflationary effects of reduced government spending and/or increased tax revenues from the *indirect* deflationary effects emanating from the reduced rate of growth of the money stock is almost insuperable. Multiple regression techniques, of course, provide a method of estimation, but in a changing economy such techniques have not been notably successful in discovering regularities so persistent as to stimulate great confidence in their results; one partial exception to this pessimistic assessment is examined and found wanting in the latter part of Chapter 7.

The fact of change in the economy is the major reason for scepticism concerning one possible proposal for overcoming this difficulty of separating out the threads in a deflationary pattern. In principle, one might suppose that a solution would be to compare developments in periods of fiscal deflation without monetary squeeze with those in periods of fiscal-cum-monetary deflation. While it would be reasonable to make such an attempt, however, it is difficult to feel optimistic about the value of the results. Any such investigation depends, not only on the availability of data adequate in quantity and quality, but also on the familiar assumption of *ceteris paribus*; the great difficulty of empirical work in economics is that *ceteris* are not *paribus* for very long. Because of this, when the results of an investigation clash with an observer's theories, it is rarely difficult to provide alternative and plausible explanations of the results. Therefore, the results tend to be accepted only by those observers whose theories fit the results. So the debate goes on, with large empirical labours making often only a marginal contribution to the outcome.

However, when that is said, it remains true that we have discovered one channel by which the conceptual principles of monetary management suggest that the authorities can successfully exert influence over the size of the stock of bank deposits. The next step in the examination of those principles must be to face a question that has so far been avoided by placing very little emphasis on the role in the economy of what we have called the o.f.i.s. Implicitly, we have followed the Keynesian convention of supposing that the distinction between banks and o.f.i.s is clear-cut, that 'liquidity' can be identified with 'money', and that credit creation is the concern solely of the banks. Many readers will be aware that this convention has been the subject of spirited controversy in the UK since the publication of the *Report of the Radcliffe Committee on the working of the Monetary System* in 1959. Obviously, any theoretical assessment of the likely effectiveness of control of the banks must await some examination of, and at least provisional judgment on, the issues in this unfinished controversy.

CHAPTER 6

Other Financial Institutions

A complex of interrelated issues is involved in the controversy concerning the nature and significance of the operations of, respectively, banks and o.f.i.s. The controversy has its chief focus on the liabilities rather than on the assets side of these institutions' balance sheets, and is sharpest in the case of those o.f.i.s whose liabilities are in some respects at least closely similar to those of the banks. In the UK we may think of building societies and hire purchase finance companies as the primary examples, being institutions that accept deposits possessing in very high degree two of the three major characteristics of bank deposits. These two characteristics are liquidity and capital certainty; except in what have been in recent decades very exceptional circumstances, the deposits of building societies and hire purchase companies can be withdrawn on demand or at very short notice without fear of erosion of their nominal (money) values. The characteristic of bank deposits that these o.f.i. deposits do not share is that of being themselves a medium of exchange, passing from hand to hand in settlement of debts; the possessor of building society deposits must exchange them for cash or bank deposits if he wishes to use his assets to finance a purchase of goods.

The controversial issues can be appreciated more clearly with the aid of our stock-flow diagram, elaborated yet further from the form reached in Fig. 5:1. We need to look only at the bottom, 'capital circuit' section of the full diagram, set out in its new form in Fig. 6:1. Because of the increased complexity of this new form, most of the channels have been labelled to facilitate reference. The main addition is the 'tank' of o.f.i. deposits (let us for convenience call them near-money, *N*), fed from current saving (channel *A*) with a counterpart in flows (*B*) of loanable funds to o.f.i.s.

Wealth-holders' liquid assets

We can break into the problem by examining the interrelationships between the volume in this o.f.i. tank and that in the M_2 tank. Here we are initially concerned with the demand by wealth-holders to hold in their portfolios stocks of highly liquid assets, available in forms that are often argued to be (cf. the first paragraph above) close

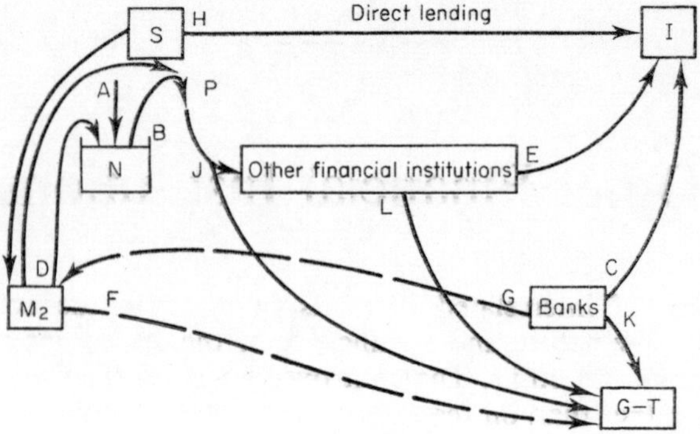

FIG. 6:1

but not perfect substitutes for each other. From the *subjective* standpoint of the asset-holder the difference may indeed be presented as extremely small; time deposits with the banks yield interest just as do o.f.i. deposits, and the additional trouble and/or expense in converting an o.f.i. deposit into bank deposit or cash form before making a payment may be almost negligible. Nonetheless, additional trouble and/or expense *is* usually involved, and we may think of the normal situation as one in which the interest yield on o.f.i. deposits is marginally higher to compensate for a very slightly smaller degree of 'liquidity'. From an *objective* standpoint that considers the contrasting effects of the use of bank and o.f.i. deposits to make payments, the difference appears necessarily to be somewhat larger. If *X* makes a payment to *Y* by transferring a bank deposit, that is that (unless *Y* exchanges the deposit for cash or some other asset); if *X* withdraws funds from a building society to finance the payment, there must be repercussions arising from the society's reaction that might well disturb quantities and/or prices in the mortgage and related markets.

Not surprisingly, there is some tendency for those inclined to stress the distinction between bank and o.f.i. deposits to emphasize objective phenomena, and for those inclined to play down the distinction to emphasize subjective considerations. Even on the subjective side, however, it is possible to produce conceptually cogent arguments for very different degrees of emphasis on the distinction. It will be convenient for us to begin by examining these differences, returning later to consider the significance of the objective approach.

The differences of view can be seen in sharpest definition by abstracting from the influence of saving flows (growth of the total wealth stock). We then have a situation in which we can suppose that a certain proportion of the given wealth stock is held in the two main liquid forms. Those who, on the basis of the foregoing considerations, regard bank and o.f.i. deposits as close substitutes in the eyes of asset-holders would then tend to visualize the asset-preference schedules in terms that recall Fig. 2:1(b). This line of thought can conveniently be labelled 'Radcliffian', since it underlay much of the analysis and prescription of the Radcliffe report (cf. paras. 312 ff.). The important aspect of the Radcliffe doctrine for us to notice is that it carries the implication (see Fig. 6:2) that restrictive monetary policy is likely to have a good deal of its potential deflationary effects on aggregate spending offset by expansion of o.f.i. credit. This implication can be argued most strongly if we think first of restrictive monetary policies that affect the cost and availability of bank loans rather than the stock of bank deposits (any decline in advances being compensated by increases in other categories of bank assets, e.g. long-term bonds).

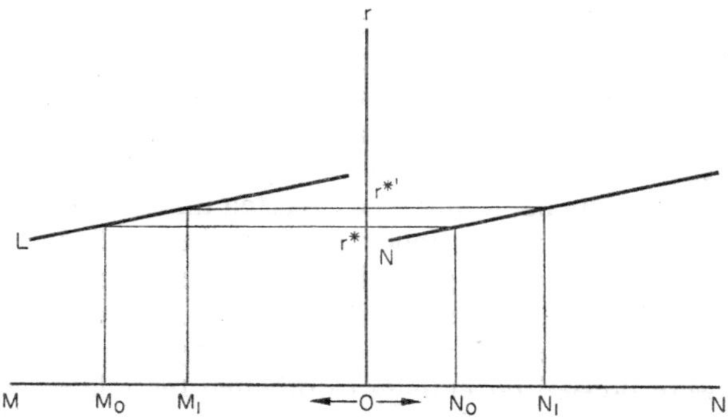

FIG. 6:2

The offset arises, as Fig. 6:2 makes plain, because the tendency for interest rates to rise ($r^* \rightarrow r^{*1}$) under the impact of a squeeze on bank credit causes asset-holders' preferences with regard to the disposition of their liquid assets to be revised in the direction of relatively lower money holdings and relatively higher near-money holdings. (Given that we regard M as including interest-bearing time deposits, a rather debatable point, the argument would require that interest rates on near-money should rise, not only absolutely but also relatively to those on time deposits. This might well be feasible if those refused bank advances seek loans from o.f.i.s, enabling these institutions to raise their lending as well as their borrowing rates, but see further pp. **000** ff. below). So we might have a smaller flow of bank loans offset by a larger flow of o.f.i. credit so that total lending to the private sector by financial institutions is maintained – to the accompaniment (it is important to notice) of an increased velocity of circulation of money balances, rather than a reduced stock; we can think of M_0–M_1 of money balances (Fig. 6:2) leaving the M_2 tank (Fig. 6:1) and being used as active balances in the income and/or capital circuits.

Reluctantly laying aside a strong temptation to oversimplify, we must recognize that rising velocity (V) of an unchanged money supply (M) is not more than half the story that a realistic Radcliffe approach ought to tell, because a general rise in short-term interest rates would in principle also tend to attract funds from idle (or compressible active) balances into government debt. Because of the pressures on the monetary authorities to prevent rates from rising too far too quickly, with the risk of destabilizing asset-preference schedules – recall the argument of Chapters 2 and 3 – the newly demanded debt would tend to be supplied from official holdings, facilitating reduced borrowing from the banks. In Fig. 6:1, we can think of positive flows along F, and possibly negative flows along G (bond sales by the banks), causing reduced M. We shall argue below that this complication is important for other reasons, but we leave it aside for now in order to concentrate on stark clarification of doctrinal differences on the significance of bank/o.f.i. relationships.

As so far expounded, it might be objected that the foregoing ideas imply only that monetary policy needs to be applied in stronger doses to achieve a given target reduction of spending in an economy with o.f.i.s than in an economy without them. For the model of Fig. 6:2 shows a stable demand function for money, and if monetary restriction were pressed far enough to threaten the idle balance stock with exhaustion, presumably the willingness to acquire claims on o.f.i.s in substitution for money balances would diminish. However, other strands of Radcliffe-type thought on these matters do suggest the likelihood of instability of the money-preference schedule of a kind inimical to the success of money supply restriction. On the one hand, intermediaries might, by changing the *quality* of their 'products' (e.g. making them more liquid) rather than their prices or yields, make them better substitutes for money than hitherto. On the other hand, the process of economizing on money balances as bank credit is squeezed is likely to be subject to a 'ratchet effect' because, for example, once firms have instituted procedures for minimizing cash holdings the procedures are unlikely to be abandoned when the bank credit squeeze is relaxed. So it can be argued that there is a tendency for the L schedule of Fig. 6:2 to move closer to the origin and for the N schedule to move outwards from the origin. Any tendency for these shifts to gather speed during periods of restrictive policy would work counter to the objectives of policy. For even if we conceive of an effective squeeze on the quantity of bank deposits (rather than on the cost and availability of bank advances), rising interest rates might by the means sketched in this paragraph still induce reduction of remaining idle balances, or economy of active balances, to finance the acquisition of new claims on o.f.i.s.

The general tenor of Radcliffian doctrine, then, is to minimize the potential effectiveness of squeezing bank credit on the grounds that, given acceptance of the idea that the demand for credit is not very sensitive to interest rates – especially in the short term, such squeezing can be neutralized by expansion of credit through other channels. In passing, it should be mentioned and stressed that increases of non-institutional credit, especially trade credit, can in principle be at least equally relevant with rising o.f.i. lending. So Radcliffe envisages (Fig. 6:1, flows) reduced lending along *C* being offset by increased lending along *D*, *B* and *E*; and also (Fig. 6:1, stocks) reduced volume in the *M* tank being offset by increased volume in the *N* tank – i.e. a tendency for LESS *M* and MORE *N* to go together. Among the many semi-helpful metaphors and analogies that have been used to render these ideas more easily memorable are the picture of the credit system as a balloon of which one end (o.f.i.s) expands as the other end (banks) contracts; and the reference to 'slippage' reducing the effects of a money squeeze on aggregate demand.

The corresponding mnemonic devices of the anti-Radcliffe position are the picture of the credit system as a concertina, the whole of which responds to pressure on one (the monetary) end; and the reference to 'leverage' tending to magnify the direct effects on aggregate demand of restricting bank credit. The Fig. 6:1 interpretation of this position implies, on the stock side, a lower quantity in the M_2 tank causing liquid asset-holders to desire *smaller* holdings in the *N* tank; and, correspondingly, smaller flows along *C* being reinforced by smaller flows along *E*. This view is clearly predicated on the proposition that *N* and *M* are to be thought of more as complementary goods than as substitutes, as thus exhibiting low rather than high cross-elasticity of demand; indeed, pressing the analogy with goods rather far, one might say that on this view *N* and *M* tend to be demanded in rigid proportions as relative prices change (cf. cups and saucers) rather than highly flexible ones (cf. two brands of petrol).

Largely because of its incorporation in some modern accounts of the Quantity Theory, we may perhaps legitimately label this anti-Radcliffe doctrine with the admittedly vague term 'orthodox'. The orthodox picture corresponding to the Radcliffian Fig. 6:2 is shown in Fig. 6:3. The quadrants are now separated because money is regarded as a *highly specific* asset possessing its own yield (an implicit 'psychic convenience yield' even if – as is usual with demand deposits – the explicit interest yield is zero). The reduction in the money supply from M_0 to M_1 is thus associated with a rise in this yield from rM^* to rM^{*1}. The effect of this rise is to reduce the desired N-stock at every level of N-yields, i.e. to shift the N-preference schedule towards the origin – so that even were the actual yield on N to rise proportionately with the yield on money, as shown, the resulting desired N stock would be lower than before the monetary restriction. In effect, transactors are depicted as reacting to the reduced money stock in part by 'cashing' liquid assets (claims on o.f.i.s) in the effort to rebuild their money balances – an effort which can be successful for individuals but not (if M were indeed under strict official control) for all transactors together. So, in contrast to the Radcliffian notion just outlined, LESS M goes together with LESS N.

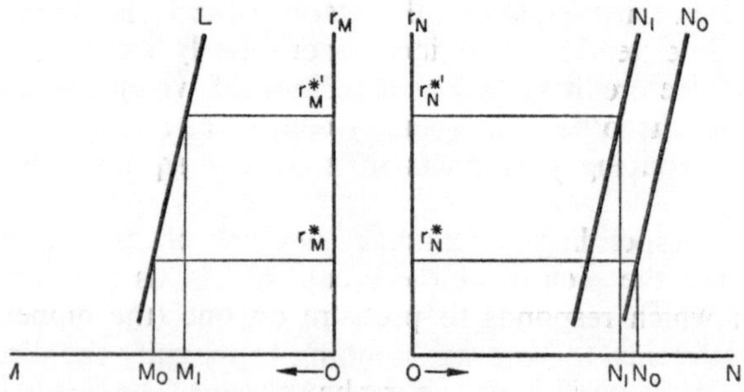

FIG. 6:3

If it be asked why empirical investigation has not produced speedy judgment between hypotheses so diametrically opposed, the answer is that here, as elsewhere in economics, the powers of empirical work are very limited. Apart from the general problems to which reference is made elsewhere we may mention now three specific problems in investigating the present issue. One is the extreme difficulty of drawing an operational dividing line between M and N which carries widespread conviction (a difficulty which, it may be noted, in itself represents ammunition for the Radcliffian standpoint). A second is that substitution across the margin between long-term assets and near-money assets tends to occur contemporaneously with the switches between money and near-money in which we are here interested, and disentanglement of the two types of substitution appears possible only to incurable optimists; pessimists are more impressed by the vast complex of influences on the markets in long-term assets, influences that would need to be explained and removed to isolate the effects of switching between such markets and the markets in near-moneys. The third is associated with the fact that, through time, the total wealth stock is growing as savings are made from income flows, so that in practice it is not at all easy to distinguish *wealth* effects on the demand for *M* and *N* from the *substitution* effects with which Figs. 6:2 and 6:3 are concerned and which are most relevant for financial policy. If, as has in fact been the case in much of the post-war period, we observe *ex post* that the *N* stock has grown faster than the *M* stock to the accompaniment of increasing wealth and rising interest rates, it is hard to know whether to attribute what is observed to differing wealth elasticities of demand for *M* and *N*, or to a high elasticity of substitution between them, or both. The difficulties are compounded when it is recognized that there is little reason to expect these elasticities to have remained highly stable in a period in which so much (e.g. income level and distribution, personal and company savings ratios, expectations of economic growth and inflation) has changed so greatly. As will become plain in the course of this chapter, other difficulties of interpretation arise when we view the operations of banks and o.f.i.s in rather more realistic, less abstract fashion than we have done so far.

Money and near-money again: the supply side

From one standpoint, the quest for greater realism requires that we should now take more explicitly into account influences on *M* and *N* from the supply side. So far we have largely restricted our considerations to demand influences (though we have been unable to discuss them entirely without mention of the action of banks and o.f.i.s as suppliers of liquid assets). Our general implicit assumption has been that the actual stock of *M* was substantially under official control, and that o.f.i.s were usually passive in accepting the volume of deposits placed with them by the public at interest rates which themselves largely reflected (given the relevant asset preference schedules) official decisions on the level of *M*. But leaving aside the question of the authorities' ability to influence or control *M* which has been one of our main concerns and to which we shall return in Chapter 7, it seems possible on reflection that these conventions (though not uncommon in debate on the significance of *N*) exaggerate the passivity of o.f.i.s as deposit-seekers. We can, then, move the argument on a stage further by examining a question that has, it will become evident, large implications for monetary policy. Looking at N and M_2 and the credit flows associated with changes in these stocks (Fig. 6:1) from the supply side, how do we conceive the interrelationships between banks and o.f.i.s? Is there any substantial degree of competition for deposits between the two groups? In particular can the o.f.i.s themselves, in the absence of restrictive official policy, do anything significant to influence the size of the total flow of funds into the finance of investment ($C+E+H$ in Fig. 6:1) and their own share in that total flow; or are they more accurately thought of as passive intermediaries providing no more than a convenient and efficient channel along which funds that would in any case have been available for borrowing flow from saving to finance real investment expenditures?

Not surprisingly, views on this larger question tend to be linked quite closely to attitudes on the narrower matter of demand conditions for M and N. And for reasons examined above, the orthodox doctrine on the larger question has tended to be that the function of o.f.i.s is indeed to be seen as that of 'pure intermediation' in the credit system, as opposed to the role of the banks as creators of credit unable to perform the intermediary function. The banks, one might phrase it in a quite useful analogy, are the manufactures of the commodity (bank deposits) in which o.f.i.s deal as wholesale and/or retail distributors. The corollary of this approach, of course, is the orthodox proposition that if the authorities want to crack down on the financial system's contribution to feeding aggregate demand, it is more sensible and effective to restrict the production of money by the banks than to devote effort to damming up the channels through which bank money flows between saving and investment.

We shall now turn to argue, from a standpoint that is Radcliffian in the sense of being in the Radcliffe tradition rather than based directly on the Radcliffe report, that this orthodox doctrine is substantially misconceived (at least in the UK setting, given the way the UK system has operated for we may suspect that Radcliffe principles have more general application but have no space to do more than glance at other environments in the present work). The orthodox position is, to recapitulate, that

(1) banks are creators of credit who cannot intermediate;
(2) o.f.i.s are pure intermediaries who cannot create.

We shall argue that this extreme position is based on a partial and incomplete analysis of financial processes; that, despite the complexity of more comprehensive analyses, the simple techniques used in Chapter 5 to integrate credit flows, real flows, and financial stocks can provide useful and reasonably realistic insights; and that, in particular, the incorporation into the analysis of the financial operations of government is essential if any significant degree of realism is to be achieved.

Credit creation and financial intermediation

We take up first, then, the orthodox doctrine that the banks are 'pure' credit creators, incapable of intermediation. This is the doctrine which underlies our having drawn Fig. 6:1 and its predecessors to show the banks as financial injectors having no direct connection with the flow of savings corresponding to the link labelled *J* for o.f.i.s; a flow of new lending from banks generates an increase in the community's stock of financial assets from the *supply* side, an increase that must be absorbed as a result of private sector reactions that serve ultimately to increase the *demand* for financial assets. The incompleteness of this analysis in a realistic framework incorporating government can be demonstrated by means of the simple model of government finance used in Chapter 5. In particular, we take up the question, left hanging earlier, of the implications of a situation in which bank deposits coming into existence as a by-product of bank loans to finance expenditure are not desired by savers as additions either to their active money balances at current income levels, or to their idle balances.

The orthodox treatment of this situation was described in Chapter 1. We recall the contention that money balances in excess of holders' requirements will either enter goods markets to call forth greater output and/or bid up goods prices, or enter financial asset markets with the effect (in the absence of previously unsatisfied borrowers who can increase the 'output' of financial assets) of bidding up the prices of existing assets and thus reducing the yields. The important point was that, because of the status of bank deposits as exchange media, there was no way in which a situation of excess supply of bank deposits to the private sector could, by that sector's own action, lead to reduction of the stock of (nominal) deposits.

This orthodox treatment can be illustrated in terms of the Chapter 5 model by recalling Fig. 5:2(c) and taking the opposite 'extreme possibility', the case of a government deficit financed by borrowing from the banks (money creation) while those who save from the incomes generated by the deficit desire to add to their bond holdings. According to orthodoxy, the outcome will be (if we stick to the pure Keynesian case in which excess money balances enter financial and not goods markets) a decline in 'bond' yields that will reduce the demand for bonds and ensure that the increment to the money stock becomes firmly held. This outcome is illustrated in Fig. 6:4(a).

In the light of our argument (Chapter 3) for the reasonableness, at least in UK circumstances, of an official policy of moderating sharp movements in interest rates, we can back the realism of a different sequence – illustrated in Fig. 6:4(b). The full implications of the latter sequence, however, will emerge more clearly if we now consciously relax the constricting assumptions of the timeless Keynesian multiplier analysis used in Chapter 5. A full treatment of the lagged case would become rather involved, and we shall avoid unnecessary complication – at the cost of some looseness of argument – by simply distinguishing between (a) an intermediate and (b) the final outcome.

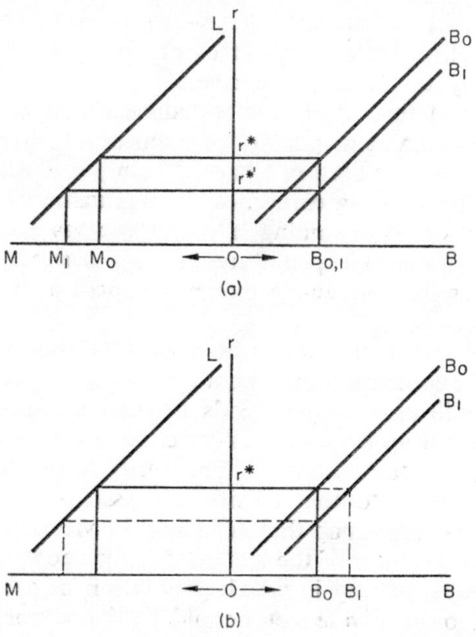

FIG. 6:4

Let us suppose, then, that a balanced budget situation such as is depicted in the arithmetical example of p. **000** is disturbed by a budget deficit lasting for only one time period, the deficit arising from increased government spending of a once-for-all nature.[1] This

[1] The fact that government spending does not continue at the higher level, of course, means that income will at first rise and then fall back again as the expansionary stimulus is removed. The exposition of the next four paragraphs traces through the events of the expansion phase, and then breaks off. This rather artificial device is necessary to avoid the extra complications of argument that would follow from other courses of action, courses that would involve setting out

deficit spending will, as illustrated in Chapter 5, generate incomes out of which there will be savings that are in principle available to finance the deficit. But it is important to realize that the unlagged Keynesian multiplier possesses a major shortcoming as a tool for analysis of financial processes in this type of situation. This shortcoming consists in a failure to explain how the increased level of spending is to be financed (as it must of course be financed) in the interval before the higher incomes that it generates have yielded corresponding increments of savings.

We have, that is to say, an 'interval of disequilibrium' in which planned injections to the income stream ($I+G$ in our model) exceed 'planned' or expected leakages ($S+T$ in our model). Various theoretical arguments have been advanced to explain the manner in which this discrepancy might be resolved. Some of these arguments involve adjustments of interest rates, as pictured in Fig. 6:5. Thus classical economic theory postulated that, even if injections (investment) were not sensitive to interest rates, then leakages (saving) might be, so that a rise in r would stimulate saving – and incidentally avoid altogether the Keynesian income adjustment process. Again, Radcliffian theory can be represented as interpreting L in Fig. 6:5(a) as a schedule showing the supply of loanable funds as elastic to increases in interest rates on account of the tendency for such increases to stimulate mobilization of idle money balances; in this case, of course, the Keynesian income multiplier would be unimpeded.

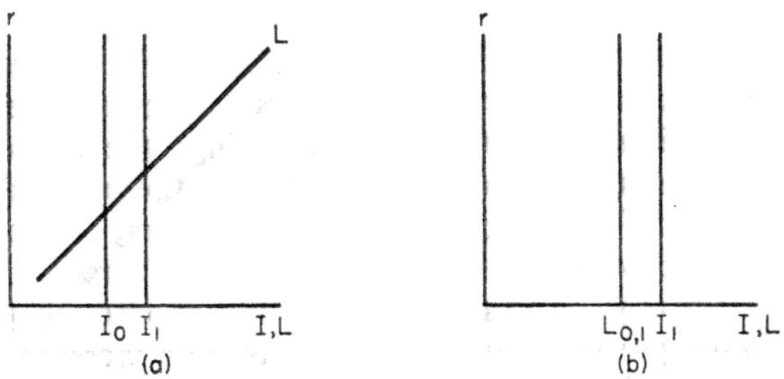

FIG. 6:5

Probably few would place much weight on either of these mechanisms in the present context, however. Saving is widely thought to be pretty insensitive to interest rates, while the time lags involved in the

a fairly elaborate model with precisely specified time lags and analysing a situation of moving equilibrium. The course adopted in the text enables the simpler comparative statics method to be preserved, and does not (the author has checked) significantly modify the conclusions of the argument.

process of mobilizing idle balances are probably too long for the process to have much relevance in a situation in which, as in our example, the government requires assured and immediate finance to cover its planned expenditure.

It follows that the situation is probably well represented by Fig. 6:5(b), in which case we can see the great importance of the banks if the financial system is to be capable of adjusting to such disequilibria without impeding real expenditure plans. For this much can be conceded to orthodoxy: that the banks *are* the only entities who possess the power of credit creation in the particular sense of being able to make loans that do not reflect purchasing power previously transferred to them by others. They need, of course, either to have reserves in excess of the minimum requirements or to have access to additional reserves; but we have argued (Chapters 2, 3 and 7) that the authorities have little effective choice but to allow them such access, especially in a situation such as that pictured in Fig. 6:5(b) where interest rates would be subject to extremely strong upward pressures in the absence of some relief from the pressure of demand for funds. And we should notice also that where, as in the present instance, the borrower is the government, the banks tend to acquire liquid government debt as counterpart to the rise in deposits, so that reserve problems are minimized. Accordingly, returning to Fig. 6:4(b), we can regard as a realistic *intermediate* stage the monetary expansion from M_0 to M_1 as the public sector deficit is financed by the banking system as residual purchasers of government debt.

Contrary to the orthodox solution of Fig. 6:4(a), however, the final outcome is likely to be quite different from the intermediate. For if, when additional income and savings have been generated, the private sector desires to add to its bond holdings, then either directly or by deflection (as described in Chapter 4), there is likely to be increased demand for government debt. However, because of the official policy of moderating sharp movements of interest rates, and perhaps additionally because the authorities consciously wish to exert downward pressure on bank deposits, this increased demand is likely to be met from the authorities' own portfolios. In this case we have (Fig. 6:1) additional flows along J that enable the authorities to redeem official debt held by the banks (negative flows along K). In the final outcome, therefore, bank deposits fall back (Fig. 6:4(b)) towards M_0, the private sector's bond stock rising towards B_1. (We say 'towards' because, though rather loose, it reflects the possibility that not all of the increased private sector bond demand will find its way, even indirectly, into government debt.)

We have now arrived at an important conclusion concerning the orthodox doctrine that the banks are pure credit creators incapable of intermediation. Our analysis suggests that they are indeed credit creators, though in the limited sense that their liabilities rise one-to-one as their assets expand, but that this is to be thought of as primarily a disequilibrium phenomenon. The banks can 'smooth' disequilibria between planned injections and planned leakages. They do so, however, by providing a flow of credit rather than a stock of assets. But in the model we have examined, the increment to asset stocks, a by-product of the bank lending flows that overcome one disequilibrium, created another disequilibrium – between the private sector's desired and actual financial asset stocks. Though we have not, indeed could not, demonstrate this point rigorously, it seems intuitively plausible that the model in this respect represents the normal case; only by coincidence would the public's ultimate equilibrium demand for bank deposits exactly equal the initial increment of deposits accompanying bank loans to finance increased spending.

In equilibrium, however, the volume of bank deposits in existence will tend to be the volume that the economy wishes to hold. That is to say that the quantum of bank loans will be limited by the economy's willingness to hold bank deposits. But this of course is precisely the same statement that can be made (and is made by orthodox as well as other commentators) concerning the quantum of o.f.i. credit. In other words, were we to confine ourselves to equilibrium situations, there would be much substance in the commonsense view that banks, just like o.f.i.s, act as intermediaries between savers and (real) investors.

Just how reasonable it is to concentrate attention on equilibrium positions is a question raising large issues into which it is inappropriate to delve very far here, because they are difficult if not impossible to solve. These issues centre around stock-flow problems that we have already encountered in various aspects. It is arguable that analysis of successive positions of full stock equilibrium in financial asset markets is of somewhat academic interest unless such equilibria are restored, following a disturbance, quickly in relation to the time horizon of interest for the particular analysis being undertaken. In this book, our primary focus of interest is on short and medium-term monetary and financial policies, implying a time horizon not exceeding, perhaps, 6–12 months. Empirical work on the length of the time lags involved in reaching desired (equilibrium) portfolio positions has been attempted, but the results to date are inconclusive, and it is not easy to be optimistic that this situation will change.

In any case, before we can judge how far to press the re-assessment implied in the foregoing conclusions, it is desirable to return to specific consideration of the o.f.i.s in relation to leg 2 of the orthodox dichotomy, which sees o.f.i.s as pure intermediaries who cannot create credit flows, and whose activities do not (in contrast to the banks) add to the private sector's asset stock 'from the supply side'.

On this point we may note first that we have already encountered one theoretically possible manner in which o.f.i.s can create credit in the rather restricted sense of a flow of loans that would not otherwise have been available. If the relative preferences of wealth-holders for *M* and *N* are more accurately depicted in Fig. 6:2 than in Fig. 6:3, and if o.f.i.s can raise their deposit rates *relative to those of the banks* (an important caveat, on which see below), then they can stimulate economy of active bank balances and mobilization of idle balances. They would thus secure command of exchange media with which to finance new loans. For a demand for loans from the private sector to exist, of course, either o.f.i.s must be able to 'bid' borrowers away from other lenders by offering cheaper credit and/or easier conditions, or there must previously have been a 'fringe of unsatisfied borrowers' of credit standing acceptable to o.f.i.s. As the former would be an unlikely development in the context of o.f.i.s offering higher deposit rates, we must here concentrate on the latter possibility.

If the o.f.i.s preserve their normal reserve ratios, some relatively small proportion of the new lending would flow to the public sector (Fig. 6:1, *L*) and thus result in redemption of public sector debt held by the banking system as residual holders, and so in a lower level of bank deposits. This apart, however, it needs to be noted that this type of credit creation by o.f.i.s, even if the conditions exist to make it feasible, implies what might be termed 'relative' rather than 'absolute' competition with the banks for deposits. For apart from this relatively small potential for reduction of bank deposits (we may note, for example, that UK building societies' liquid reserves in public sector debt tend to vary in the region of 15 per cent of total assets), the process here examined results in more o.f.i. deposits but *not* in less bank deposits – rather, as we have seen earlier, we get increased velocity of circulation of an unchanged stock of such deposits. On the other hand, we may also recall the previous argument: if rising o.f.i. rates have a tendency to pull up short rates generally, then there may be flows into government debt along channel *F* (Fig. 6:1), resulting in further downward pressure on bank deposits.

However, we must move on to notice a gap in the argument of the last two paragraphs and a mechanism that might link expansion of o.f.i. credit and consequent flows into government debt in less marginal ways. For this purpose, we need to follow up the possibility just mentioned that the o.f.i.s – having attracted existing bank deposits – find new borrowers from among transactors previously unable to secure credit. Such transactors may then be pictured as using their newly secured credit to make income-creating expenditures that are a net addition to the total. In this case, the o.f.i. expansion will have touched off an income expansion process; from the new incomes, savings will be made that must be 'placed' in financial or real assets.

Given the available 'menu' of assets and the pattern of yields, it is to be expected that some part of the new savings will find their way along *P* (Fig. 6:1) into o.f.i. deposits, so that we would have a process that might without undue violence to linguistic convention be called an 'o.f.i. credit multiplier'. It is difficult to think that this multiplier would be very large. The reader can check for himself that, with the multiplier model of Chapter 5, an o.f.i. stimulated expansion of aggregate demand by 100 units would raise income by 250 units and saving by 50 (so that for the 100 expansion of demand to be maintained, o.f.i.s would have to mobilize a further 50 of bank deposits by competitive bidding). If the 'marginal propensity to place savings in o.f.i. deposits' were 0·2, then the 'feedback' to o.f.i.s at the next stage would be only 10. In this connection, however, we recall our arguments that, on a realistic view of the working of the UK system, any bank credit multiplier effects are also extremely small.

But we must also realize that the existence of a 'marginal propensity to place savings in government debt' requires that the argument be taken a stage further. For suppose we take this propensity as 0·5, which is not wildly unreasonable since public sector financial liabilities in the UK have been computed at over 40 per cent of total financial liabilities, so that the *average* propensity approaches half. Then, on the above figures, we would have a flow into government debt of 25, and reduction of public sector borrowing from the banks by like amount, even in the absence of any bank credit multiplier effects.

When to this potential reduction in bank deposits is added those suggested in the last paragraph but three, it seems reasonable to argue that an o.f.i. credit expansion, while it may start by mobilizing existing bank balances, may be the time of the attainment of final equilibrium in income flows and asset stocks, having given rise to quantitatively significant reduction of the bank deposit total (though there would probably be other contemporaneous upward pressures on bank lending and deposits, so that this reduction will be relative, compared with what the total 'would otherwise have been'). If this be accepted we have arrived at a theoretical mechanism with some claim to realism by which banks and o.f.i.s are seen to be competitors for deposits in the 'absolute' sense – MORE o.f.i. deposits implying LESS bank deposits, and thus tending to the support of 'Radcliffian' rather than 'orthodox' expectations.

It is important to be clear, however, that this competition is rather indirect, and in fact reflects as it were a three-sided competition for funds between banks, o.f.i.s and the public sector. However, *if* it is accepted as reasonable to concentrate attention on equilibrium positions rather than on continuing shifts from one disequilibrium to another, then one might summarize the foregoing argument by saying that it seems nearer to a complex truth to think that the relationship between banks and o.f.i.s is one of straight competition for funds in much the same way as would happen if bank deposits were not media of exchange. Suppose, for example, that only cash (Bank of England notes and coin) were directly transferable; then we would think of banks and o.f.i.s as competing against each other for deposits of cash. More realistically, we may conjecture that in course of time the public in the UK might come to rely on the National Giro for providing a payments mechanism, using the banks and the o.f.i.s as repositories for short-term savings; in this situation, which approximates to the present position in some European countries (e.g. Germany) few would deny the validity of the idea that banks and o.f.i.s were competitors for such savings.

There is, however, one further step before this section of the argument is complete. We need to return to the caveat in parenthesis on p. 179. The general tenor of the exposition so far has carried an implied emphasis on o.f.i.s as potentially[1] powerful competitors of the banks on account of an ability to raise their deposit rates relatively to those of the banks. This emphasis is perhaps significantly Radcliffian, the Radcliffe report having been written with direct reference to UK conditions. The aspect of these conditions relevant in the present context is of course the 'cartel' arrangements by which the UK clearing banks maintain their (time) deposit rates at a common

[1] The *potential* nature of o.f.i.s competitiveness with banks in the UK perhaps needs a little emphasis. Attention is often drawn to the fact that the biggest single non-bank group of institutions taking short-term deposits on a 'retail' scale, the building societies, do not behave in the manner analysed in the text. Against this, however, it may be said that the main groups of deposit-takers at the 'wholesale' level, non-clearing banks and hire purchase finance companies, *do* operate competitively on interest rates; and also that there is a possibility, as yet untested, that the building societies tend to use non-rate methods (such as advertising) to try to influence their fund inflows at various stages of the cycle. But there are conceptual arguments concerning whether non-clearing banks are best thought of as banks or as o.f.i.s. And so there is room for argument about how far o.f.i.s as a group in fact behave in ways that might result in restriction of bank credit being offset because o.f.i. credit is 'higher than it would otherwise have been'.

level fixed in relation to Bank Rate. In this situation, if o.f.i.s bid higher rates for deposits they are insured against retaliation by the clearing banks unless consequent or concurrent inflationary developments stimulate the authorities to raise Bank Rate.

In so far as the UK group of clearing banks do compete for deposits, therefore, they do so with one arm tied behind their backs though it is occasionally and temporarily unloosed by administrative decision of the authorities. They are restricted for most of the time to fighting with the other hand, representing competition in the provision of services. Here what is perhaps their main advantage, the direct and easy transferability of their liabilities in debt settlement, has been gradually whittled away in the post-war period as o.f.i.s have moved in the direction of quicker and easier withdrawal facilities for depositors. The relative loss of ground by the clearing banks is hardly surprising. (We may note in passing, however, that as business entities they have substantially offset this loss by entering the o.f.i.s' field of business by taking over hire purchase companies and operating them as separate subsidiaries.)

An interesting contrast emerges if we glance at the situation in the United States. There the commercial banks were also 'docile' in the 1950s, but have changed their policy to one of aggressive price competition for deposits in the 1960s, with results of which we have already had occasion to take brief notice. The conclusion seems to be that when the banks fight with both hands *they* are the powerful competitors, capable of doing serious damage to the o.f.i.s unless the referee steps in. And this is not really surprising, for the banks do have many competitive advantages in price-*plus*-services competition. On the price side, their lending rates tend to be more flexible than those of o.f.i.s particularly o.f.i.s engaged in mortgage business. On the services side, the banks can add widespread branch networks and favoured access to overdraft facilities to the easy transferability inducement.

So, with docile banks and dynamic o.f.i.s, the authorities would be well advised to consider ways and means of bringing o.f.i.s within the sphere of monetary control, as the UK authorities have in fact tried to do in the 1960s. With dynamic banks, the authorities are more likely to find their main problem in keeping the banks in subjection without producing widespread disruption of the financial system. But either way, to talk of competition between banks and o.f.i.s is to undermine at least the more *simpliste* versions of orthodoxy, which deny the possibility of such competition on the grounds that the volume of bank deposits is determined by the volume of reserves made available to the banks by the authorities and by the relevant multiplier coefficient.

Putting together these critiques of the two legs of the orthodox dichotomy between banks and o.f.i.s, we can see that there are considerable grounds for arguing that the similarities between the two groups of institutions outweight the contrasts. If the argument were accepted, then in visualizing the flows through the financial system in the manner of Fig. 6:1, it would be more (even if not totally) realistic to eliminate the separate treatment of the banks; to place them in the o.f.i. box to form one group of financial intermediaries; but to recognize that, for the sorts of reason we have discussed, these intermediaries are not entirely passive links between current saving and current investment.

Cyclical changes in financial institutions' portfolios and their consequences

There is, however, one further reason for emphasizing the non-passivity of all financial intermediaries as a group, and we must notice it before we close our examination of the operations of intermediaries in the context of Fig. 6:1. From time to time in the foregoing discussion we have stated or implied a simplifying assumption that, when new lending resources accrue so that assets can be expanded, banks and o.f.i.s expand their existing asset categories in proportion, leaving the ratio of each individual asset to total assets undisturbed. This simplification seems reasonable for abstract theorizing, but it should be noted that there is evidence to suggest that it is unrealistic in one particularly important respect.

We can best examine this aspect in the context of the investment cycle of four to five years' duration that can be detected in post-war UK data. Figures for the later 1960s have been subject to policy influences stimulated primarily by balance of payments pressures in (by the standards of the first two decades post-1945) abnormal degree. But in the middle 1960s there seems to have been a reasonably well-defined cycle in investment by the UK company and personal sectors, with a peak in 1964. The relevant figures are set out in column 1 of Table VI. (The figures are rounded to the nearest £100 million. The source and definitions are given as an earnest of good faith, but it will come as no surprise to any reader who has attempted to use financial statistics to learn that the table is constructed on the basis of very rough-and-ready treatment of the inadequacies of the published data. In particular, it might be mentioned that in dealing with lines 23 and 24 of the data, the attempt has been made to exclude second-hand deals in company securities by the heroic simplification of taking the figures for new issues only and assuming that the whole total was taken up by financial institutions. The general pattern of the table is not much affected by this manhandling of the figures.)

Table VI. *Investment and lending in the mid-1960s (£100m)*

	1 Investment by UK company and personal sectors	*2* Company and personal borrowing from financial institutions	*3* Financial institutions' lending to the public sector
1962	3,000	1,200	600
1963	3,300	1,500	400
1964	4,300	2,100	–100
1965	4,200	1,700	900
1966	4,000	1,500	500

Source: Bank of England *Quarterly Bulletin*, December 1962, ('Sector Financing Accounts, 1952–66').
Definitions: col. 1 – lines 2, 3, 4; col. 2 – lines 16–19, 23; col. 3 – lines 6, 12, 15, 20–22.

For the types of reason just hinted at in the parenthesis, data affording a comprehensive picture of the sources of finance for the investment totals given in column 1 are simply not available. But column 2 picks out companies' and persons' borrowing from financial institutions, so far as the statisticians have been able to track it down. It will be seen that such borrowing shows a close tendency to rise and fall with investment as here defined; indeed the *proportion* of investment represented by borrowing from financial institutions is higher at the cycle peak in 1964 (almost half) than near the lower turning-points in 1962 and 1966 (around two-fifths).

If we ask how financial institutions were able to provide this cyclically varying total of loans, we might expect to find the main answer in corresponding cyclical fluctuation of their deposit and other liabilities. But the figures for these accruals (not here presented because of considerable complication of analysis and presentation) bear this out in only limited degree. The main answer that does emerge from the data is summarized in the figures in column 3 of the table, which show that (aside from 1965 – mentioned below) the institutions' lending to the public sector had a strong tendency to vary *inversely* with their lending to the private sector.

How the public sector accommodated itself to such large fluctuations in one particular source of funds lies outside our main present concerns, but by way of rounding out this rough sketch we may mention that the main offset was that the public sector's sale of reserves to, and borrowing from, overseas residents fluctuated helpfully. When, in 1965, this source of funds failed to fill the 'autonomous' gap between the public sector's needs and available borrowings, the sector made exceptional use of 'created' funds from the banking sector – borrowing from the Bank of England and by sale of Treasury Bills to the banks.

What this all amounts to in terms of Fig. 6:1 is easily stated. The flows E/C into the finance of investment appear to have varied cyclically with investment and therefore, by presumption, with the demand for external finance by private sector investors. Whether this cyclical variation has been due to relative profit considerations, or to some institutions giving priority to private sector borrowers, it was possible (in 1962–6 at least) because flows L/K varied anti-cyclically. That is to say, there is evidence of 'switching' of lending channels by financial institutions of a type tending to ensure that private sector borrowing demands are met.

The public sector was saved from embarrassment due to this switching partly by the autonomous operations of the system (domestic expansion – external deficit – financial accruals to the authorities) and partly by resort to the banks as residual lenders. So we come back to the main issue between orthodoxy and what we may perhaps call the 'Radcliffism' of this book, which is whether the authorities have any effective choice open to them of causing the system to operate differently. To this more severely practical question we now turn.

CHAPTER 7

Conclusions

In this closing chapter, an attempt will be made to draw together the main strands of the foregoing exposition, and to present some conclusions. More specifically we shall be attempting to use some of the insights gained in the detailed discussions of Chapters 2–6 to provide a basis for some evaluation of opposing general conceptual approaches of the kind examined in Chapter 1. An adequate treatment of these approaches would require a separate book, but the obligation to attempt to clarify the broad implications of the details of our argument is one that cannot and should not be evaded.

We have been engaged in analysing the potentialities, during periods of strong pressure of aggregate demand upon an economy's productive potential, of a restrictive monetary policy directed primarily at easing demand pressures by influencing the quantity of money – of which quantity we have assumed bank deposits to be the dominant component. The mainstream, orthodox assumption based on economic theory of banking has been that such influence is relatively easy to achieve in a developed financial system in which the commercial banks hold their liquidity reserve wholly or primarily in the form of claims upon the central bank. For these claims represent the central bank's liabilities, the volume of which will vary as the central bank causes its holdings of assets to vary by buying and selling securities, that is to say, by open-market operations. With commercial banks operating on a fractional liquidity reserve basis, such operations will tend to result in the impact effect on bank reserves in absolute terms exerting a multiple effect on bank deposits and the money supply.

The very fact that this theory of changes in the money *supply* can be described without reference to the private sector's *demand* for money balances underlines what is analytically much the most significant feature of orthodoxy concerning monetary management, viz. the notion that the money stock is correctly regarded as being determined EXOGENOUSLY, so that the economy has no choice but to adapt itself to a money stock over whose size it has practically no control. Once given this vital feature, then debate concerning effects of policy-induced changes in the money stock centres on the nature of the economy's demand for money balances and the responsiveness of that demand to different influences, of which theory has tended to concentrate on income (and/or wealth) on the one hand, and interest rates on the other. However, while this exclusive emphasis on stock aspects is useful in abstract theorizing, we argued in Chapter 1 that a realistic conceptual framework would only be achieved if the flow implications of changing stocks were constantly borne in mind.

In Chapter 1, for purposes of getting the argument off the ground reasonably quickly, the standard textbook Keynesian framework was used, with only a side glance at criticisms of that approach. Against that background, however, we can now usefully review a wider range of theories, broadly in order of their historical development.

In the broad sweep of history, Quantity Theory approaches to monetary analysis have certainly been dominant. The tendency of such approaches has been to emphasize the medium of exchange function of money, and therefore the dependence of the demand for money balances upon the size of the flow of income and transactions, requiring the use of money, period by period. Accordingly, if from an equilibrium position the money stock were exogenously increased, the process by which the economy adapted itself to this increase would be that of expanding demand for *goods* rather than that of expanding demand for *securities*.

On this theory the central bank is clearly very powerful. For we see that it adds to the bank credit multiplier notion of a close causal relation running from central bank liabilities ('high-powered money') to the quantity of commercial bank deposits, the further notion of a close causal relation running from the quantity of bank deposits to the flow of aggregate demand.

This second notion, of course, implies that the velocity of circulation of money or deposits is highly stable. More recent developments of the Quantity Theory, due primarily to Professor Milton Friedman, present a picture that is rather more complex in detail though not different in essentials. The demand for money is argued to depend on the level of *permanent* income (roughly, the sustainable trend level, which can be regarded as rising slowly through time as the wealth stock increases) rather than on the level of current, *measured*, income which can fluctuate a good deal around the developing trend. It follows that an exogenous expansion of the actual money stock that causes expenditures and measured income to rise will not immediately affect the size of the desired money stock. Spending will therefore tend to increase further, i.e. velocity of circulation will tend to increase; gradually, however, as the community's perceptions of the level of permanent income are adjusted upwards, the desired money stock will rise and velocity will tend to fall back again. Thus velocity is not static, but it varies in a systematic fashion.

The Quantity Theory, then, sees the demand for money as strongly related to income, and weakly related to interest rates. By contrast, Keynesian analysis rests on the assumption that both income and interest rates are important influences. The income-related ('active balances') demand is thought of as being satisfied first, however, with the interest-related ('idle balances') demand occupying a residual position. From this follows the idea that exogenous changes in the money stock initially affect the supply of idle balances, i.e. the change in the money stock is prevented from affecting expenditures by an offsetting change in velocity of circulation in the opposite direction. thus a rise in the money stock is 'neutralized' by a fall in velocity. However, the fall in velocity will be accompanied by a decline in interest rates and *if* spending is interest-sensitive, aggregate demand and income, and the demand for active balances, will increase: velocity tends to rise again.

In this context, the power of the central bank is problematic. We still have the close causal relation between high-powered money and bank deposits. The link between bank deposits and spending, however, is indirect and *possibly* weak; for example, if spending is not very sensitive to interest rates.

Radcliffe-type monetary theory goes a stage further in developing scepticism concerning the powers of the central bank. For here (cf. Chapter 6) emphasis is placed on the existence of close substitutes for money, which have the effect of making the demand for money highly sensitive to interest rates, so that quite large exogenous changes in the money stock would have relatively small effects on interest rates and thus (for any given interest-sensitivity of expenditures) on aggregate spending. The uniqueness of money as an exchange medium, which is the foundation of the Quantity Theory, is recognized but argued to be of relatively trivial importance. In the absence of money holdings, an individual's spending can be financed by sale of non-monetary assets, particularly short-term assets whose capital value is more or less certain. Alternatively, spending can be financed by borrowing, especially by the issue of short-term claims which holders of existing money balances can be induced (by offering only small premia over existing market rates) to substitute for money balances in their portfolios. Thus with a given money stock, velocity of circulation will respond rather passively to changes in aggregate demand for goods.

All of the foregoing arguments can be derived from very abstract textbook models which treat the demand schedules for money and other assets as highly stable and simply argue about their shapes. However, we noted earlier that Keynes himself talked a good deal about the possibility that volatile expectations in a world of uncertainty concerning the future might cause the liquidity-preference schedule to shift bodily from time to time. With a given money stock, such shifts would of course cause interest rates to fluctuate even in a Radcliffian environment of highly interest-elastic (static) schedules.

In the world of textbook models, fluctuating interest rates can be regarded with intellectual curiosity but with complete equanimity; especially if demand for goods is not very interest-sensitive, nothing much happens. The core of the argument of this book is that, in the real world in which central bankers actually operate, fluctuating interest rates cannot be regarded with anything like complete equanimity. Further, the argument as we have traced it in Chapters 2–4 suggests that central bank attempts to operate an orthodox restrictive monetary policy would themselves tend to generate interest rate fluctuations.

These arguments require, however, yet further elaboration before their force can be fully appreciated. For one thing, we have for convenience of exposition used mainly the framework of a static economy with a given wealth stock. But it would clearly be more realistic to revert as in Chapter 1 to considering the case of an economy growing through time with a wealth stock that is growing.

Such an economy is well described in Keynesian terms as one in which planned investment exceeds planned saving, so that if we continue to assume that all investment is financed externally – or alternatively that a given proportion of investment is so financed – then *planned borrowing exceeds planned lending*. Now it is true that Keynesian thought envisages such a situation resulting in an income multiplier process that raises income and saving, but such increases take time to materialize; and in a consistently growing economy, the discrepancy between the demand for borrowed funds (= supply of securities) and the supply of borrowed funds (= demand for securities) will persist. We have also noted that Radcliffian reasoning suggests that the discrepancy might be eliminated as rising interest rates induce mobilization of previously idle money balances, and that such a process can in most circumstances go some way before the increased cost of borrowed funds serves to moderate the desire to undertake real investment. The point to be established, however, is this. In a growing economy, the 'natural' environment of central bank action is one in which interest rates are tending to rise because of excess demand for loans, quite apart from any influence that price inflation might have on the willingness of holders of 'second-hand' bonds to continue holding them unless the money yield rises to maintain the real yield.

There is, however, one source of relief for the discrepancy between planned borrowing and planned lending that does not involve rising interest rates: cf. the argument of pp. **000–0**. Those institutions whose deposit liabilities circulate in settlement of debts (in the UK, the clearing banks, but not the so-called 'secondary' or merchant banks) can make loans that do not depend on someone have previously transferred purchasing power to them, can 'create credit' – *provided* that as their loans and deposits rise they have access to increments of reserves to enable them to maintain their reserve ratio(s).

From all this it follows that the effective choice facing a central bank in an economy displaying buoyant, expanding demand with inflationary pressures is between:

A attempting to prevent the expansion of bank lending and bank deposits, acquiescing in a 'Radcliffian' credit expansion outside the banks that is marked by increased velocity of circulation of money balances and rising interest rates; and

B holding its hand, allowing bank lending and bank deposits to rise, meanwhile passively supplying the banks with reserves or turning a blind eye as the banks acquire them elsewhere (cf. the American banks' borrowings in the Eurodollar market in 1969).

The implications of the central bank choosing course A need to be examined further, for there are difficulties additional to those already noticed. We might realize first that, in a 'tight money' situation (declining ratio of money supply to GNP at current prices), not all transactors are motivated to act in ways that serve to increase the 'physical' circulation of money. In particular, we might say that those deficit units (investment > savings) who cannot easily switch borrowing channels when bank credit tightens, have an incentive to maintain turnover by delaying settlement of debts (taking more trade credit).

We note secondly that tight money and rising interest rates present long-term real investors with a temptation to make do with temporary finance by issuing short-term claims to transactors who have funds to spare for a short-time – floating long-term bonds can be virtually impossible while interest rates are rising and bond prices falling. Again we can turn by way of illustration to the US, where in 1968/9 bank credit squeezes and bond market paralysis were accompanied by enormous expansion of company borrowings from other companies in the commercial paper market. When such short-term promissory notes mature, companies that have put such funds to illiquid uses need to refinance the debts; this can be difficult if a deterioration of market confidence has reduced their credit-worthiness, which could well happen if delayed cash receipts (cf. our previous point) have, or are rumoured to have, damaged their liquidity position.

Thirdly, we recognize that these several possibilities of deteriorating confidence in the ability of borrowers to meet their obligations have particularly potent implications for the equity market. For this is a market whose fortunes are especially closely tied to the confidence in the future felt by investors who seem to be predominantly 'risk averters' (i.e. to be deterred by possible losses more than they are attracted by possible gains of equal size), and to be subject to contagious waves of optimism or pessimism when (possibly fortuitous) conjunctures of events happen to augur well or ill for future yields or prices.

When these considerations are put together with those discussed in earlier chapters, we have assembled an outline of the case for the view that a central bank that opted strongly and consistently for policy A in a growing economy with deep-rooted inflationary pressures would be courting the risk of serious disruption of financial markets. It would not be a matter of gentle pressure on the monetary brake producing a diffused willingness of deficit units to make marginal reductions in their borrowings and expenditures, reducing planned investment in relation to a given (or even increased) level of planned saving; nor of a squeeze on the liquidity of asset-holders inducing mild rephasing of spending plans. Rather, it would be a matter of acquiescing in conditions that might stimulate asset-holders to a radical reshuffling of portfolios in the direction of liquidity – more specifically, in the direction of holding claims that were both capital-certain and free of risk and default; a reshuffling that could for a time render well-nigh impossible the raising of external finance by companies, who are incapable of issuing such claims.

The use of the conditional tense in these last two sentences is deliberate, for it can be asserted with some assurance that no central bank has opted consistently for policy A in the post-1945 world of growth and (increasingly) strong inflationary expectations. Rather, what we have had is a rather narrow range of policy approaches with at one extreme Japan, seemingly (and – increasingly from about 1965 – the US) operating policy A tentatively and temporarily, switching rather hastily to policy B whenever the gathering clouds threatened to break into a storm. And, at the other extreme, the approach in the UK of pretty consistent adherence to policy B combined with various attempts at selective control of particular credit flows. (The Bank of England's later very cautious experiments in the direction of policy A described earlier in a period when it is arguable that a radical change in the stance of *fiscal* policy had the effect of moderating the demand for external finance, do not really call for a substantial qualification to this generalization.)

Although the argument of this book has necessarily concentrated on the UK institutional setting, there is, as we have just hinted and as argued in the appendix to Chapter 2, evidence to suggest that it is of considerable relevance (*mutatis mutandis*) in other developed financial systems. We have noted evidence of its operation in the US. That the same basic dilemma, arising from conflict between the 'support' and the 'control' functions, shows up on systems possessing very considerable institutional differences, suggests strongly that we are here concerned with an enduring fundamental of central banking rather than with an institutional peculiarity of a particular country during a particular period.

Among the many differences mentioned in the appendix to Chapter 2 and elsewhere, we can recall the following. The United States banking system contains thousands of separate banking entities, while the United Kingdom system consists of a small number of banks with extensive branch networks. US banks have, at least since the early 1960s, operated in a highly competitive manner in bidding for deposits by interest rate competition; the UK banks have competed in the provision of services, but have maintained an interest rate cartel agreement by which rates have continued to be linked more or less rigidly to Bank Rate. The US banks do not adhere rigidly to *minimum* reserve ratios, and there is a flourishing market (the so-called Federal Funds Market) in which reserve balances at the Federal Reserve banks (the central banking system) are traded between banks with excess reserve holdings and those with reserve deficiencies; the UK banks do observe rigid cash ratios, and their sense of immediate dependence on the central bank in case of reserve difficulties (albeit at one remove via the discount market) is thereby sharpened. In the US the proportionate weight of public sector debt in the total of claims traded on financial markets is perhaps only half of the UK proportion. Despite these and other differences, one recent quantitative investigation of Federal Reserve policies concluded that in the post-war period only 'about one-fifth' of policy actions were made in pursuit of what we have called control objectives, while the remainder served (in our terminology) support functions.[1]

However, central bank action to support the financial system along the lines of policy B consists essentially of action to moderate fluctuations in interest rates because of the ways in which such

[1] M. Keran *and* C. Babb, *Federal Reserve Bank of St Louis Review*, July 1969.

fluctuations can damage the viability of the system. To moderate fluctuations in interest rates is very far from being the same thing as to stabilize interest rates. But the effects of a central bank policy of 'leaning into the wind' on interest rates are not only to reduce the amplitude of 'natural' fluctuations, but also to slow down the speed of movement. In an evolving, changing economy, to slow down the speed of change is to affect the system in a way that is quite well represented by visualizing complete stabilization of rates in the more easily handled static textbook model. If the (stock) demand for money is interest-sensitive, then such models show that interest rate stabilization results in the size of the money stock varying in accordance with changes in the demand for money (Fig. 7:1). In the 'real world', if holders of government securities know that any substantial rise in interest rates will not be allowed to occur very quickly, they know that time will be available in which to turn such securities into money without incurring very significant capital losses.

So we reach the conclusion of Chapter 6 that in practice, and in equilibrium situations, there is much to be said for treating the money stock as an endogenous rather than an exogenous quantity.[1]

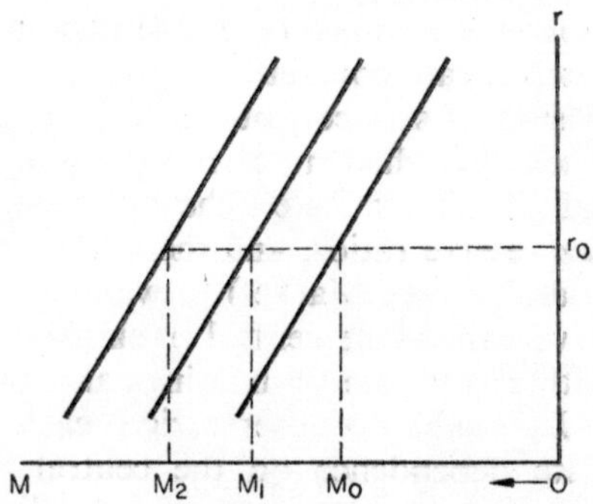

FIG. 7:1

This does not mean that the authorities are always powerless to achieve influence on the size of the money stock in a particular direction. For, on the one hand, autonomous changes in market expectations might sometimes shift asset-preference schedules in a

[1] It is this central conclusion of our whole argument that explains the absence in these pages of discussion of the thorny question of the correct operational definition of money. Such questions as the inclusion or exclusion of time deposits, and of non-clearing bank deposits, are of concern to those who regard it (a) as very important and (b) as practicable to exert close control over the nominal stock of money. Readers desiring guidance on these questions might usefully consult an article by E. V. Morgan in *The Manchester School*, September 1969.

manner consistent with a change in the money stock being achieved *without* substantial fluctuations in interest rates. And more importantly, on the other hand, the authorities can use *fiscal* policy (Chapter 5) to 'nudge' asset-preference schedules in a desirable direction, and can well hope that the straight economic effects of fiscal action will be reinforced by a psychological expectations shift; thus, in an inflationary situation, a severe fiscal policy that succeeds in reducing spending and incomes directly will tend (a) to reduce the demand for money balances, e.g. because of lower transactions needs, and (b) to induce expectations of a downturn in interest rates that will cause a shift away from preference for liquidity in asset structures and increase the demand for interest-bearing assets.

But acceptance of the notion of a considerable degree of endogeneity of the money stock implies scepticism not only of the orthodox view of monetary management underlying all existing types of approach to macroeconomic theorizing. It also implies scepticism in particular concerning the fundamental Quantity Theory notion of 'a close causal relation running from the quantity of bank deposits to the flow of aggregate demand'. For if the size of the money stock is, in important degree, responsive to the economy's demand for money balances, it is not easy to see why changes in the size of the money stock should be capable of forcing the economy, in the aggregate, to modify its spending decisions.

The grounds for this scepticism are not in the least affected by the econometric evidence frequently advanced in support of the Quantity Theory, evidence that shows a rather consistent cyclical pattern in which changes in the money stock 'lead' changes in activity/prices, the latter following money changes with a somewhat variable time lag. For there is no difficulty in advancing explanations of this pattern that are more obviously compatible with the view that changes in the money stock are (primarily) induced by changes on the side of the demand for money rather than by policy-imposed changes on the supply side. For example, a Keynesian account of events during the cycle upswing might first emphasize the inception of the upswing in 'autonomous' changes in spending propensities, secondly hypothesize that early increases in expenditure were financed primarily by borrowing from banks with associated increase in the money stock, then thirdly visualize the multiplier process of income expansion proceeding to the accompaniment of rising velocity of circulation of a no longer growing quantity of money.

It is true that our argument in Chapter 6 suggested that in the second of the foregoing stages, marked by an excess of planned investment over planned savings, the central bank might be able to create some impediments to the expansion process by limiting the ease with which the banks could provide (a flow of) finance for the excess investment. Not all spenders have easy access to alternative financing channels in the manner emphasized by Radcliffian reasoning, and in any case the process of adaptation to bank credit stringency must take a certain amount of time. However, in this connection the evidence that financial institutions tend to give priority to private sector borrowers during periods of buoyant demand and expectations becomes very relevant. The total (stock) of bank credit might be successfully limited, for a time. But unless such limitation is pressed far enough to provoke a liquidity crisis, the effects on expenditures are likely to be very limited. For if the banks accommodate private sector credit demands by raising their advances ratios, and if o.f.i.s similarly switch towards emphasizing private sector lending, then the demand for government debt declines, the banks as residual holders take up more government debt and the money stock tends to rise. Because of effects on interest rate expectations, the decline in willingness to hold government debt will be stronger the harder the central bank presses its initial restrictive actions, so that the support duty casts its shadow in advance and inhibits central bank control policies even before it becomes an immediate and unavoidable constraint.

So we reach the general conclusion that, in attempts to stabilize the economy in situations of excessive aggregate demand, quantitative monetary policy is a weak tool, although, as an adjunct to fiscal policy, it can perhaps make some (probably marginal) contribution ('Monetary measures can help, but that is all . . .' – Radcliffe report, para. 514). In general, the monetary and financial system is adaptable and responsive to the economy's financial needs, and the central bank's power to alter this situation by market methods is very limited unless it is willing to risk a liquidity crisis. In situations of *deficient* aggregate demand, when stabilization policy calls for spending to be stimulated rather than restricted, this technical impediment resulting from the central bank's support duty is of course much less immediately pressing, though it is a long-established doctrine that a central bank is wise to prevent future difficulties in advance by avoiding encouragement to the development of potentially unstable and vulnerable credit structures. In any case, the argument that 'business wags finance' rather than vice versa implies that the central bank's power to *induce* (as opposed to permitting) credit expansion is also a very limited one. For here the importance of the stress laid in this book on realistic conceptions embracing flow as well as stock implications of monetary change again becomes relevant. If money dropped like manna from the skies, an increase in the money stock might induce a rising flow of spending. If money expands as banks lend, then monetary expansion cannot occur in the absence of a demand for (a flow of) loans. This conclusion is only superficially modified by recalling that bank deposits can be increased by bank security purchases in, for example, the bond market. For, by and large, the bond sellers will be financial institutions, who in turn will be unable to touch off a net increase in loan-financed expenditures in the absence of 'a fringe of unsatisfied borrowers'.

It thus appears that monetary policy using the subtle, indirect methods of open-market operations is weak and circumscribed, whatever the stance of general macroeconomic policy. But in the excess demand situations with which we have been primarily concerned, there is in principle more hope for direct controls on lending flows. If finance can be denied to borrowers through one channel (e.g. bank advances), we have noted that there are limitations on the ability of some borrowers to switch to borrowing through other channels. And if some of the other channels can also be (at least temporarily) blocked up as well, then spending might well be reduced for a time. The analogy has been drawn between such a 'credit squeeze by directives' and a bomb that blocks a city's main traffic routes. After a time, traffic finds other ways round, but temporarily the total flow of vehicles through the city is reduced.

It is not surprising, therefore, that central banks have tended frequently, in the face of feelings of impotence to control the *money stock* by *market* methods, to resort to attempts to control *credit flows* by means of directives. But in this direction, too, various difficulties and disadvantages are encountered. For a variety of historical and structural reasons, it is the major commercial banks who are most amenable to control by directive (or by 'moral suasion' backed up by the implied threat to use directives to secure compliance if necessary). But to control the big commercial banks alone is to give competitive advantage to 'fringe banks' and o.f.i.s to whom frustrated bank borrowers are likely to turn. To control a wider spectrum of established institutions is to give competitive advantage to small lenders and/or new lenders who slip through the net of control. The approach might achieve some success, at a cost in terms of unfairness and reduced economic efficiency that is judged worth paying if the excess demand/inflationary situation is short-lived. But, in face of the prolonged inflationary pressures of recent years, the attempt to sustain controls of this type over a considerable period is likely to meet with increasing resentment and resistance.

The foregoing paragraph summarizes adequately the experience of the Bank of England during the post-war period as it has reacted to circumvention of control of clearing bank advances by widening the scope of requests and directives to include hire purchase houses, merchant banks and building societies. In face of the complexities and frustrations encountered, it is understandable that the superficially simpler, narrower monetary approach embodied in the domestic credit expansion concept has had attractions apart from those of satisfying the country's international creditors. If the argument of this book is correct, however, the authorities cannot guarantee to stay within a highly restrictive d.c.e. ceiling unless fiscal policy is appropriately deflationary.

The use of a monetary ceiling to ensure the adoption of an appropriate fiscal policy is the true novelty of the d.c.e. device. But in many respects the new policy looks like a resurrection and up-dating of the old ceiling on the fiduciary note issue. Both systems have tried to tie internal monetary expansion to balance of payments experience; both have reflected suspicion of the proclivity of governments to avoid the political unpopularity generated by taxation by resort to monetary creation. The rigidities of the old system caused difficulties that resulted first in its emasculation and ultimately in its abandonment. Unless the workings of the financial and economic systems have changed in a very fundamental way, we shall in due course witness a further demonstration of the dictum that those who ignore history are condemned to repeat it.